THE SEVEN DESIRES OF EVERY HEART

Also by Mark and Debra Laaser

Healing the Wounds of Sexual Addiction by Mark Laaser

Shattered Vows: Hope and Healing for Women Who Have Been Sexually Betrayed by Debra Laaser

THE SEVEN DESIRES OF EVERY HEART

MARK & DEBRA LAASER

ZONDERVAN®

ZONDERVAN.com/
AUTHORTRACKER
follow your favorite authors

Requests for information should be addressed to:

Zondervan, *Grand Rapids, Michigan 49530*

Library of Congress Cataloging-in-Publication Data

Laaser, Mark R.
      The seven desires of every heart / Mark and Debra Laaser.
         p.   cm.
      ISBN 978-0-310-27816-0 (hardcover, jacketed)
      1. Spiritual life—Christianity. 2. Spiritual formation. I. Laaser, Debra, 1951- II. Title.
BV4501.3.L325   2008
   248.4—dc22   2008024286

Interior design by Beth Shagene

Printed in the United States of America

08 09 10 11 12 13 14 • 24 23 22 21 20 19 18 17 16 15 14 13 12 11 10 9 8 7 6 5 4 3 2 1

To our children, Sarah, Jonathan, and Benjamin,
who God has given us and entrusted us with the opportunity
to serve the Seven Desires of their hearts.

CONTENTS

ACKNOWLEDGMENTS

Every book has a journey. Some books start with the wounds of their authors and the healing journey they have discovered. Such is the case with this book. This book's journey began in 1987, when we were a very broken couple. We were referred to a therapy center in a simple and unpretentious place. We had driven past this modest building many times but had never noticed the small sign "New Hope"—nor had we ever thought about needing some of that for ourselves. We had no idea we were going to meet two of the finest therapists we've ever known. Tom and Maureen Graves began serving us in ways that left us wanting more. Yearnings of our hearts were being met in that modest place, and we were growing emotionally and spiritually. Over the years of working with Tom and Maureen and of finding hope for ourselves, the ideas that formed the basis for this book developed.

Tom and Maureen were students of one of the greatest therapists and teachers of the twentieth century—Virginia Satir. Even though we never met Virginia, through Tom and Maureen we feel as though we know her. We owe a great debt of gratitude to her work. It was her model in those early days that showed us that our problems were only symptoms of deeper desires. As we discovered our own desires, the model of the Seven Desires began to take shape.

At first, we took what we were learning home to our own family. As parents of three precious children, Sarah, Jon, and Ben, we began to see that underneath their problems were also deeper unexpressed emotions and desires. In our own imperfect parenting, we tried to serve their desires. We are grateful to them for their patience with us as parents. We are so proud of the young adults they are today. We are also extremely gratified to see how sensitive they are to the desires of others.

In the ongoing journey of this book, God has continued to bring to us many hurting people. In every case they would come to us with a behavior that was creating crises in their lives. We are thankful to those that trusted us long enough to help them discover the deeper desires of their hearts underneath these behaviors. We know that it takes a commitment not to look for a quick fix. It also takes a willingness to do the hard work of lasting change. We wish we could name all of them. Their stories are what we hope make this book more relevant to the reader. They are the ones who helped us finally name the Seven Desires.

Over the years a number of churches have invited us to present the material in this book. We thank every one of them for giving us the opportunity to test our ideas. We also thank them for their encouragement and prayers. We especially thank Dave Trautmann at Westwood Church in Minnesota for all of the time he spent helping us incorporate the Seven Desires material into the couples' ministry of that church.

Through some work we did with the International Bible Society, we met a man who is himself a writer and editor. Pat Springle graciously volunteered his time to review the manuscript, and he made invaluable suggestions.

Every book's journey has those who have encouraged it in a

variety of ways. Jennifer Cisney was one of the first to tell us that this material was worth developing. Gary Gray and his staff at Gray Communications helped us in some of the early formulation of our teaching. Bob and Johna Hale of L.I.F.E. Ministries have been enthusiastic about this material since we first began talking about it. Mary Munger interpreted the "stances" with her professional artwork. Mike and Linda Richards, Elizabeth Griffin, and Dave Carder have all in their own way supported us.

Finally, the journey of this book has been prayerfully encouraged and supported by the entire Zondervan family. For the last fifteen years, we have been blessed to know our editor, Sandy VanderZicht. This is the third book of ours she has graciously shepherded through completion. Thanks, Sandy, for affirming us, choosing us, and including us in your work.

MARK AND DEBBIE LAASER
Eden Prairie, Minnesota
September 2008

INTRODUCTION

*Our lives are shaped
by the things we desire.*
THOMAS MERTON

We believe that God created us with seven basic, universal desires. Each of us desires to be heard and understood, to be affirmed, to be blessed, to be safe, to be touched, to be chosen, and to be included. Having and fulfilling these desires validates our very existence. If these basic desires are fulfilled, we will enjoy a deeper and richer relationship with God and with others.

God put the seven desires deep inside our souls for good reasons. When we understand our desires and realize that they are the same for everyone, we can live in deeper and more meaningful community. Finding our commonalities draws us toward one another. Giving and receiving these desires allows us to connect with each other in truly intimate ways. Understanding our desires also helps us discover our true need for God. He is the only One who can truly satisfy our desires at the deepest level of our soul.

But there is a problem with our seven desires. They are so deep in our souls we don't always consciously understand that they are there. We feel them in our hearts, and we ache for them to be fulfilled, but we don't know the source of that ache. Instead of accepting the fact that we have pain and loneliness because our desires are unfulfilled, we lead lives of quiet loneliness and frustration, lives laced with anger and bitterness. We hurt and we long for something more, but we often don't even know what that "something more" is.

Often, we look to our relationships to fill us up. It is not wrong, of course, to expect fulfillment and happiness from our closest relationships—but we run into trouble when we ask those relationships to do too much. In this book, we want to suggest, first, that God is both the creator of and the ultimate fulfillment of these seven desires. Second, only when we look to God first to fulfill our desires can we then also find our desires met by other people. When we look first to friends and family to fulfill our desires, we are setting ourselves up for disappointment. But offering our desires first to God frees us to also have our desires met by other people, and to meet their desires too.

Before we go further, let us tell you a little bit about ourselves. We have been married for thirty-five years, having originally met in high school. Mark was trained as a pastor and counselor. He worked in his field for fifteen years until he was intervened on for sexual addiction and went to inpatient treatment. When Mark returned home from treatment, we both committed to counseling for ourselves individually as well as for our marriage.[1]

We were referred to a local therapist, Maureen Graves, who had been trained personally by Virginia Satir. Satir has been considered by many to have been one of the greatest family therapists of all time. Mark remembers his first session with Maureen. He was frightened and ashamed that Maureen would judge him for his moral failures. After telling her his story, she said to him, "Mark, to do all of those things, you must have been in a lot of pain." Maureen had already begun to use Satir's model with Mark. For Satir, the problem is never about behaviors; it is always about deeper issues that create that behavior.

Over the years as we have worked with Maureen, we feel extremely blessed that she was our therapist. Through her we felt like we got to know Virginia Satir, even though we never had the privilege to meet her. The ideas of this book are based in large part on the foundation of Virginia's work as we have sought to incorporate it in our own lives. Today as we work with hundreds of other people, we have continued to develop it in light of our own Christian faith.

We created Faithful & True Ministries twenty years ago so that through our counseling, teaching, and writing we might help other people find spiritual and emotional growth. This book is, in some ways, a debt of gratitude to the work of Virginia. Through Maureen, she taught us to understand our own desires. Here, we hope to help you do the same.

In this book we want to teach you several things. First, we want to help people understand the seven desires—the desires to be heard and understood, to be affirmed, to be blessed, to be safe, to be touched, to be chosen, and to be included—and we want especially to make clear that they are common to both men and women.

Second, we want to help people see how childhood and adult life experiences teach them about their desires and about getting them met. If you did not have the desires met in your childhood, you may find unhealthy ways to get them met as an adult. We will show how this happens and what it looks like when it does.

Third, we want to help you reclaim the truth about yourself and your desires. God made you as a unique and wonderful treasure. God loves you and intends for your desires to be fulfilled. God himself is the source of that fulfillment, yet he often works through other healthy people to provide your desires.

Fourth, we want to teach you how to help other people have their desires met. This is a form of service. We are called to serve, and when we do, we will also be served.

At the end of each chapter, we offer some points to ponder. These are suggestions about how to think about the information you've just gained, but you don't have to do them in order to understand the book. However, pondering these points will help you digest the information and make it more personally applicable to you.

God loves you, and he calls you into relationship with him. He has put the seven desires in your heart to show you how to have that relationship. As Psalm 37:4 puts it, "Delight yourself in the LORD and he will give you the desires of your heart." When you know this, you can find healthy ways to get your desires met, and you can serve the desires of others.

As with any of our books, speeches, or counseling, our constant prayer is that our words be instruments of God's truth. May that be so as you read on.

THE SEVEN DESIRES

Delight yourself in the LORD
and he will give you the desires
of your heart.
PSALM 37:4

What are the seven desires? In this chapter we will describe each of them. But first, remember that the seven desires are universal. *All* of us have *all* of them. Whatever your age, gender, culture, or religious background, your desires are the same as everyone else's. As you read through this chapter, try to think about times in your life when you felt your desires were being fulfilled and times when they weren't. Ultimate fulfillment in life is the result of having these desires met as well as having the opportunity to serve the desires of others.

THE FIRST DESIRE: To Be Heard and Understood

Think back for a minute to a time when you felt someone was truly listening to you. Maybe it was your mother, listening to you when you were seven as you described being teased on the playground. Maybe it was your new girlfriend, hanging in rapt attention as you talked about your family. Maybe it was your best friend, listening as you shared your fears about having a baby. Whoever it was, didn't you feel that he or she truly cared about you?

We have so many things to say. We are born to communicate. And yet so often we feel that we are not being truly heard. You know the feeling—you're trying for the umpteenth time to tell your husband about some frustration or need or desire, and he just doesn't seem to be listening. He just doesn't get it.

For many of us, our assumptions about being heard or being ignored are rooted in childhood. Think back to kindergarten, or fifth grade, or your junior year of high school. What was your experience of being heard—or of not being heard? Your parents may have been the greatest and most loving of people, yet perhaps they were often stressed or busy and didn't seem to have time to listen. Did you hear words like "Later" or "Don't bother me"? Maybe you heard, "That's a stupid thing to think" or "It's not Christian to talk like that." Many children have adults in their lives who talk *to* them —give advice, admonish them, teach them. But they don't have adults that want to listen to their feelings, needs, struggles, or opinions.

If you had a childhood in which people talked to you—or worse, at you—but never really listened, you may have given up on talking. Now, as an adult, you find that you can talk about superficial matters, but you may be unpracticed at talking about what is really going on inside of you. When your sibling or spouse says, "You never talk to me," you have no clue what they mean. You have no practice in talking, much less in being heard.

Yet we all desire to be heard. Sometimes our desire to be heard literally causes us to speak differently! When we want to communicate something important and feel we are not being heard, we might raise our voice, thinking that if we talk louder, maybe we will finally be heard. Often, people who yell and scream are really people who are desperate to be heard.

Alternately, if we want to be heard, sometimes we might say something more slowly. We might assume that the person we're talking to is just too dumb to get it. So we repeat ourselves, slowly. We say things like, "Let me spell it out for you."

And sometimes when we don't feel heard, we talk quickly — we've got a whole lot to say and we need to get it in! We hate to give up control of the conversation and we never finish a sentence, stringing together phrase after phrase with "but, and, ah, you know, so . . ." We often don't want to give up control of the floor until we feel we have been heard.

Then there are those of us who simply repeat what we're saying over and over and over. When we do this, we talk a lot. One of our friends often says, "He likes to talk a whole lot more than I like to listen."

At times we can also get overly rational and argumentative. We say things like "you always" or "you never" and then cite examples and every historical evidence of why we're right. We call this "case building" because we are building our case to prove our point. Since we want to be heard and understood, we feel that we need to justify what we are saying. The problem with case building is that it forces whoever we're talking to into defending their case or interpretation. In the face of our lawyer-like arguing, they either shut down, or they too build a case using examples and justifications. The result? We get an argument, usually a very reasonable one, in which no one is really listening to the other. Both sides come out frustrated and not feeling like they've been heard or understood.

Sometimes, in our efforts to be heard we regress — resorting to strategies that we learned early in our lives. What do children do when they want to be heard? They don't have the ability to reason yet — they may not even have language skills. So they cry or scream, plead, stomp, hit, pound, bargain, or use any other dramatic behavior to get attention. Believe us, we've worked with couples who act like three- or four-year-old children! Adults are capable of having tantrums just like children. Those tantrums are simply attempts to be heard and understood. The problem is, of course, that tantrums don't work. Instead, they alienate others, who wind up simply wanting to get away from this immature behavior.

How can we be heard by others? Ironically, one of the first steps in being heard is to listen. In order for us to connect, we must first be willing to listen. Over the years we have been to numerous seminars about how to be better communicators—which when simplified, really means being better listeners. We have been taught to be active listeners, to not interrupt, and to repeat back what we heard so that we can be sure we got it right. We have been taught to mirror each other, to look into each other's eyes, and to truly know each other.

Sometimes, the people we care about the most are often the ones who seem to have the hardest time hearing us. (Conversely, sometimes we have a difficult time listening to those we love the most.) When we are invested in a relationship, our own emotions often distract us from truly listening, even if we have the best of intentions of doing so. Great listening skills get trumped by our desire to be heard ourselves! And so we interrupt, or interject our own opinion, or figure out a way to get the focus back to our feeling, need, or opinion. It is a difficult cycle to change, for we all selfishly need to be heard and understood.

To complicate the issue further, *really* hearing someone always involves more than just understanding facts or issues. Listening involves hearing the heart of someone—hearing someone's feelings. In our counseling practice, we've found that very few people have the skill to identify, much less share, their emotions. Learning to listen to others' feelings and thoughts and to share our own will increase our intimacy with one another.

We also desire to be heard by our God. He wants us to talk to him, and we want him to listen. The Psalmist says, "I cried out to God for help; I cried out to God to hear me" (Psalm 77:1–2). In addition, God wants us to hear him: "Give ear and come to me; hear me, that your soul may live" (Isaiah 55:3). In order to connect with God and with each other, we must talk to God and to each other—and we want to know that both God and other people hear us, because being heard is a clue that we are fully known.

THE SECOND DESIRE: To Be Affirmed

How good it feels when someone says to us, "Nice job, good work, way to go, that was wonderful." How good it feels when someone says, "Thanks." We all desire to be affirmed and to believe that someone approves of who we are and what we do. Think back to the people in your life who have had the most positive influence. Were they the people who criticized and belittled you, or the people who affirmed and praised you? We suspect that the people who had the most positive influence affirmed you—and the people who belittled you actually had a quite negative influence.

We long to have parents, friends, teachers, and mentors in our lives who also notice what we do well. These are the people who, when we are young, represent God's love to us. If they are not affirming, we do not learn to feel confident in our talents and abilities. Tragically, many children not only lack affirmation, but are criticized and put down—an *anti-affirmation*, which is doubly destructive. People in our lives provide the feedback we need to develop our self-awareness about how we are *doing* in the world. Affirmation tells us that we are doing well and to keep it up. Criticism tells us we have messed up. Is it any wonder that we lose sight of God's real truth about who we are if we receive constant messages that we have failed?

Think about how many times you have asked yourself, "What do others think of me?" Some of our earliest memories are about what others' opinions of us are. We walk into kindergarten frightened and alone. We look around to see if the other children smile at us and want to play with us. That quest for welcome and affirmation continues throughout our lives, in school lunchrooms, in classrooms, on sports teams, at dances, and as adults, in neighborhoods, at work, and at church. What an experience it is when we find a church fellowship where people seem friendly, inviting, and accepting!

Our need for affirmation is so great that sometimes we refuse to try new things, because we are scared we will look foolish and be judged and criticized. Sometimes you may be afraid to talk in a group for fear that you won't say something right. Or maybe you don't get involved in learning something new for fear that you will look awkward. Or maybe you have given up on a dream you have because you can't do it perfectly. Isn't it refreshing when you take a risk to say something or do something, and despite the outcome, you are still accepted and affirmed for your effort?

And when we do make mistakes, it can be difficult to talk to people about those mistakes because, again, we fear that we will be judged. This can lead to isolation and loneliness — after all, we have all made mistakes, and part of the desire to be affirmed is the desire to be affirmed as struggling people in process, people who are loved despite our errors. Without the safety of knowing that we will be accepted and affirmed despite our mistakes, it can be difficult to ever confess our mistakes — to friends, or to God.

You may have grown up without much affirmation from your family, schools, friends, or churches. Or perhaps you grew up with lots of criticism from the same places. You wound up feeling that you just can't get anything right and that you will never amount to much of anything. You go through life feeling guilty and afraid. You may even take on responsibility for circumstances you didn't really cause. When you wind up with this kind of ongoing self-doubt and guilt, people might as well not give you affirmations, because you won't believe them anyway. Someone might say, "That was a good job," but you reply, "Yes, but . . ."

When you are desperate for affirmations you may try anything to get them. Have you ever said to yourself, "If only I could do . . ." or "If only I had . . ." You might wish for musical talents, athletic ability, or a high-powered position at work. You might think that money, a beautiful house, a new car, fashionable clothes, or some other material possession would make you acceptable to other people —or would at least distract other people from your flaws. You always have something in mind that would make you "better" and more likeable. Then others would know you're a good person and give you lots of affirmations.

Because of your desire for affirmation, you may work hard to please others. If you can just figure out how to do more, do it better, or do it differently, then people will like you, or, at least, not dislike you. Anxiety can figure into this mix. One of the greatest anxieties any of us has is the anxiety that we will be all alone in the world. Others will simply not like us, think we're deficient somehow, and then leave us. When you're like this, you will go way out of your way and bend over backwards to please. You will say to yourself, "Please don't leave me. Think of all the wonderful things I do for you."

When you live without affirmations or with lots of criticism, you develop self-doubt and guilt. "I guess I never get anything right." "If I were a better wife/husband, our marriage would be better." Self-doubt and guilt eventually lead to anxiety. Check yourself on your own levels of anxiety. How often in a given day do you find yourself wondering what someone else thinks of you? Or what you need to do to please someone else?

When it comes to those who are really close to you—family and friends—the anxiety becomes more pronounced. These are the people that you are the most afraid of losing. You might do anything to please them. This kind of anxiety leads to what we call "intimacy disorder." This simply means you have a hard time being yourself or telling the truth around those you love the most. You are trying to put your best foot forward, and you want to please. When you feel that you have pleased those you love, you have a perception that they will be happy with you and won't leave.

Concern about affirmation often manifests itself in one of two ways. First, lying. Rather than tell the truth, even to people you love, it can seem easier to evade a conversation or change the topic—or tell out-and-out lies. Maybe you started telling lies when you were young when you were afraid of what your parents would think or do if you told the truth. Maybe their reactions were, in fact, overly critical or even dramatically negative. Telling lies might have been one of the ways you learned how to survive. If you said the "right" thing, then you might not be criticized or rejected. This kind of situation created an early anxiety about how your actions affected others, and you have been on hyper alert ever since.

A second way that the need for affirmation can manifest itself is perfectionism. People who have been criticized excessively or denied affirmations often just keep working more diligently in hopes that they will finally get affirmed. If you can never get it right or you are seeking to be validated for your skills and talents, you just might develop a compulsion to work at something to achieve the unachievable. If you find yourself always needing to do more, or never quite satisfied with what you do, you may be battling the fallout of a lack of affirmation in your life.

Think about times in your life when you have grown and prospered. No doubt there was a teacher that was encouraging you, a coach that was building up your skills, a friend that was believing you could do anything, or a parent who never gave up on your efforts to follow your dreams. Having someone thank you, believe in you, encourage you, or like what you are doing promotes growth.

Our souls deeply desire affirmations. Think how often you may have wondered, "Does God really love me like the Bible says he does?" To know that God does love us and that he bestows his grace upon us is a life-transforming awareness. It gives us confidence in ourselves and our abilities. It helps us know the value of what we can do. It makes us long to serve such a God, and it makes us long to serve others. God's love and affirmation for us leads us to his calling, plan, and purpose for our lives.

THE THIRD DESIRE: To Be Blessed

While affirmations are about what we do, blessings are about who we are. A blessing happens when someone lets you know that you are a very special person in their life. They love you, they are proud of you, and they want to be with you. When we get blessed, we believe that we are special in someone's eyes. When we are blessed, we don't have to do anything; we are loved for being just who we are. It is a great feeling!

Pause for a moment, and think of your parents. Parents should be the primary and first source of blessing. Were they the kind of people who blessed you? Did they let you know how special you are to them? All of us desire to be blessed by both our mother and father. Boys look to their mothers to be blessed in their manhood just as they look to their fathers. Women, also, look to their mothers to be blessed as women just as they look to their fathers.

Those of you who are parents, think of it this way: Is there anything your child could do to stop you from loving them? They may make awful decisions and do painful things, but a parent's love is timeless—if there is blessing. If you find that you have had trouble feeling this way about a child, could it be that you feel that you were never blessed by one or both of your parents? It is hard to give what we have never been given.

When we don't receive affirmations, we can feel *guilty about the things we do.* When we don't receive blessings, we can feel *shameful about who we are.* Guilt is the awareness that I *made* a mistake. Shame is the feeling that I *am* a mistake. Shame is a powerful and destructive force in people's live. It tells us that we are bad and worthless, that no one loves us as we are, and that no one will take care of our needs. We feel that we don't deserve to have needs or desires, because no one would meet them anyway. So we go through life beating ourselves up and putting ourselves down.

Those of us who were not blessed as children often go through life silently angry or sad. Feeling angry about not being blessed is understandable, but that anger can lead you to many destructive acts against yourself and others. Anger can make us sarcastic. It can lead us to taunt people we care about. It can even lead to bursts of physical violence.

You may also feel incredibly sad if you have not been blessed. You have missed an important part of the gift your parents were entrusted to give you. You live with a handicap of sorts when you are not assured of your blessing. You are never quite sure that you are enough, that you are valuable and have purpose. You may not really identify why you are so sad or depressed all the time. But in your heart, you know there is something missing.

Another tragic result of missing out on the blessing is that you often feel like a victim—someone without choices in life. If you don't believe that you are worthy, then you will probably also deny that you have a right to have needs or desires. And when you sacrifice taking care of yourself and subject yourself only to the needs and desires of others, you feel trapped in your life with no choices. Your *feelings* of being a victim, in other words, can lead you to *become* a victim.

Alternately, you might respond to your lack of blessing with a sense of self-sufficiency and even martyrdom. If you are a martyr, you believe that no one will come to help—you must do it all yourself. Deep below the independence and self-sufficiency of a martyr lies the saddened soul of someone who doesn't know that they are worthy enough to receive help.

When we confuse the desire to be affirmed and the desire to be blessed, we wind up thinking that the way to get blessed is to do things. When you feel this way, you feel that there is some way to earn the blessing—that accomplishments, awards, acquisitions, and accolades will bring the blessing. While you may get affirmations for all these things, they don't bring you a sense of blessing. Remember, blessing is about who you are, not what you do. A part of your soul wants to know that you are valued for yourself, not for what you do.

Indeed, this desire to be blessed may be our deepest, most primal need—to know that if our accomplishments, our fame, our honors, our possessions were all stripped away, that we would still be loved simply because we *are*.

When you have received blessing in your life from your parents, your self-esteem will develop. You will feel good about who you are. You will feel loved. When self-esteem is intact, you will be less likely to be tossed about in life by what others say about you or by their behaviors. You will live more confidently in this truth.

God blessed his Son. When Jesus was baptized, a voice from heaven said, "This is my Son, whom I love; with him I am well pleased" (Matthew 3:17). Isn't it interesting that God blessed Jesus before Jesus had actually done much—he hadn't worked any miracles yet, or performed any healings. Yet God was already well pleased with him! When God says that he is pleased with Jesus as his Son, it is not because of anything he has done, but because of who he is.

As children of God, do we not also long for the blessing of God: "This is my son or my daughter with whom I am well pleased"? God has put this desire in our hearts because he wants us to know that he *is* pleased with us. We all do both good and bad things. God's love for us is never based on what we *do*. It is based on *who we are*: his beloved creatures. He made us and he is pleased with us.

So let us say that to you: you are innately good. You are worthy, and loved, just for being who you are.

THE FOURTH DESIRE: To Be Safe

We all desire to be safe—to be free of all fears and anxieties. We want to know that we are materially secure—that we have food, and a place to live, and enough money to support ourselves. We want to know that we are spiritually safe—that our God is a God who will not pull the rug out from underneath us, that he is a God who keeps his promises. And we want to know that we are emotionally secure, that those around us are reliable, that those people who say they love us can be counted on to act lovingly.

When the desire for safety is met, we feel a certain freedom and confidence to explore the world and even take a few risks. We all know people who feel wholly secure. We think of our friend Susan. Susan didn't grow up rich, but she grew up in material comfort, knowing that her basic needs would always be met. She grew up with parents who loved her, and siblings she was actually good friends with. And she grew up in a healthy church—sure, during adolescence she had the usual doubts and angst, but she never really doubted the love of God. And now, as an adult, Susan feels free—free to take risks, quitting a secure job and opening a business from home. She feels free to be generous with other people (she probably gives away a higher percentage of her income than anyone else we know). She even feels free to get angry with God sometimes, knowing that he can handle her emotions, and will love her no matter what she's throwing at him.

And then there are the rest of us. Maybe you didn't grow up in a financially secure family. Maybe you grew up with an abusive parent who couldn't be counted on to provide for your emotional needs, let alone your financial needs. Maybe you grew up in another country, where the basic rights and freedoms most Americans take for granted were up for grabs. If you grew up in a financially unstable home, you may, later in life, feel not only envy of the Susans of the world—you may feel resentment! Why do the Susans have it so easy? Why is everything handed to them on a silver platter? But that resentment may just be the desire for safety, turned inside out.

At some level we all want to be safe. We all want to live long and productive lives. We can be anxious about our health, whether or not we have food and shelter, or whether we will have enough money to live that long, comfortable, and productive life. Deep in our souls, we know having people around is safer, and so we can get anxious about being all alone.

Sometimes problems we had in the past lead us to have undue concern for our safety. Mark had a serious car accident in college when he was driving on a snow-covered road. Today, if he is driving and it starts to snow, his survival brain signals danger because it remembers that past accident. His anxiety can sky-rocket even though the roads are relatively safe.

Sometimes past trauma continues to affect us today. Some sex abuse survivors are unable to have sex with their loving spouses because even loving, intimate touch reminds them of the pain of abusive sex in the past. Mark once went up to a friend who had served in Vietnam and tapped him on the shoulder. The next thing Mark knew, he was on the ground. His friend's stress response had been so finely tuned that he snapped; at a gut level, he feared for his physical safety.

For others of us, the desire for safety manifests itself in less dramatic ways. We worry about—we even obsess about—things that are really not that big a deal. If you're like Mark, you might fixate on keeping the outside of your house just so: in the fall, you want to get the leaves raked as soon as they fall; in the winter, you worry about shoveling snow; in the summer, you want to keep the grass at a certain height. When all of those things are taken care of, all is right with the world.

Some people worry just as much about the inside of the house. Do you obsess about cleanliness or the laundry? We know one woman who spends time every day combing the fringe on her oriental rugs so that it goes in the same direction. Do you ever need to line things up, put them in order, or double and triple check whether or not you locked the doors and shut off the lights? Do you need to control *something* when many other areas of your life just feel out of control? Do you ever get mad at someone else who doesn't seem to worry about these things as much as you do? Do others ever bug you by saying things like, "Why do you worry about that so much? It is not a big deal." Frustrating, isn't it?

Our desire for safety can also lead to a paralyzing relationship with money. Most of us think that there is a certain amount of money that would finally allow us to feel safe. That amount is usually more than what we currently have! Have you ever said, "If I only got that raise, saved just a little more, or didn't have so many bills, everything would be all right"? Maybe you fantasize about get-rich-quick schemes, or even winning the lottery. Maybe you worry about money so much that you try to control every penny. Or maybe you avoid the worry and try not to think about money at all. Sometimes a penny pincher marries someone who refuses to think about money at all—and then they fight about money all the time.

Debbie came from a family that was very responsible about money. Mark came from a pastor's family that didn't have as much money but rarely seemed to worry about it. Mark remembers that it was generally considered unfaithful to worry about money, as "God always provides." Besides, if you needed something, you just asked somebody for it. That's what pastors did. Imagine what it was like for us coming together. Debbie expected Mark to manage money as well as her father had, and Mark expected Debbie to be more trusting, just like his dad was. Debbie worried about money overtly, and Mark tried to not think about it. We used to fight about balancing the checkbook. If we received an overdraft statement in the mail because Mark had forgotten to balance the checkbook, a war could ensue.

Ultimately, we discovered that Mark's spiritual attitude about money and Debbie's skills in managing it actually complemented each other. Our core messages about money came from the stories of our families, but today we can strive to create our own balance and thereby our own story. How we used to handle money illustrates that two people can have very different approaches to managing their anxieties. Each one may have a different management strategy and can, potentially, argue about why the other one doesn't share it.

People worry about their health, and they worry about money. But the anxiety of being alone is the most serious worry. All of us long to be safe in relationships. That longing can lead us to worry that someone will leave us. Do you worry about whether someone you love will love you back? Do you ever find yourself doing something to try to control their love for you? Debbie has talked to numerous women who have made decisions to be sexual with their spouses, even when they have been extremely hurt or feel very angry, just so they will be loved and not left. What lengths will you go to, even denying your own wants and needs, to please someone else so that they won't leave?

When we are controlled by our anxieties, we rarely say what we really feel. Our radar is out continually for what someone's reaction is going to be, and we are always anticipating what we need to say or do to have the safest effect. Have you ever smiled in response to something you found disagreeable because you worried about what would happen if you disapproved? If someone has asked you, "What would you like to do?" was your response, "I don't care; what would you like to do?"

In any relationship our desire to be safe may override our desires to serve and love. Our survival self is very powerful. We figure out ways to manage our anxiety, to control relatively insignificant things, health issues, money, and people. Our rational brain knows better most of the time. By the time this part of our brain catches up, we may be frustrated by our own anxiety. We can get anxious about being anxious.

God put the deep desire to be safe in our heart because he is trying to teach us to rely on him to keep us safe. Psalm 55:22 says, "Cast your cares on the LORD and he will sustain you." Jesus says in Matthew 6:27, "Who of you by worrying can add a single hour to his life?" God is trying to teach us to trust him and his promises. He is also teaching us to trust others to provide for us some of the things that will make us safe—and to serve others and help them feel safe too. As we learn to identify the ways we want to feel safe, we can invite those who care about us to be compassionate about our feelings too. When those around us cannot always give us what we need and we cannot provide even for ourselves the safety we desire, we are taught to turn to God with all that is in our heart.

THE FIFTH DESIRE: To Be Touched

Have you ever watched a newborn baby? They cry and cry until they are picked up and held, and often just that skin-to-skin contact seems to comfort them. That desire to be touched stays with us throughout our lives. That's why a hug from a coworker is a great pick-me-up in the midst of a stressful day. It's why we hold hands at funerals. Our bodies are wired to desire this touch: a recent study by scientists at the University of North Carolina found that people who hug a lot have a lower risk of heart disease!

The desire to be touched has two forms of expression. First, we all have a desire to be sexually touched. That is a part of our human nature, and God put it there so that we will be fruitful and multiply. Second, we all have a desire to be touched in nonsexual ways. A problem arises when these two desires get confused.

The desire for sexual touch is the energy inside of us to be productive, passionate, and creative. It is a life force that leads us to reproduce, build things, and invent new solutions to life's problems. This drive, in other words, is much larger than just the act of sexual intercourse. It is the source of our passion and all things creative in us. The sex drive is not evil, but it can be expressed in sinful ways when we don't follow God's design for healthy sexuality.

Have you ever wondered why we can be attracted to lots of people and yet God commands us to be abstinent before marriage and monogamous in marriage? It doesn't seem fair, does it? Countless numbers of people deal with sexual temptation every day. We live in a sexually saturated culture. Everywhere you turn, you find advertisements, songs, and images that challenge us to be more sexually active. Research suggests that as many as two-thirds of all men and one-third of all women have looked at Internet pornography. For many of the people we work with, sexual activity has become an addiction.[1] Think of the famous artists, actors, politicians, and even religious leaders who have struggled with sexual issues. The same creative, passionate, and productive side of them that makes them so successful also makes them more vulnerable to sexual temptation.

The answer, we believe, to this deep biological drive is to express it in the context of a spiritual and emotional covenant called marriage. When a husband and wife are spiritually and emotionally connected, physical passion takes on a whole new dimension — it becomes an expression of spiritual and emotional intimacy, not just a passion to be satisfied for purely physical release.

The spiritual connection in marriage is what satisfies the biological desire in us all. That is the way God made it and is why he commands us to be sexual only in marriage. Only a one-flesh union can fulfill the true spiritual nature of sexuality, and only marital sex can truly be satisfying. Furthermore, when sex in a marriage is not satisfying or fulfilling, emotional and spiritual disconnections are occurring.

The second form of the desire for touch is the desire for nonsexual touch. We all have a desire to be touched skin to skin, and this kind of touch doesn't have to lead to sex. There are very powerful chemicals in the brain, such as oxytocin, that get released when we experience skin touch, and those chemicals give us a sense of well-being that is essential for us to grow and prosper. Think of what happens to babies when they don't get enough touch; they fail to thrive and might even stop growing. If they are severely neglected, they might even die.

Once we were on a plane flying home from Korea. On the same plane was a proud set of parents who had just adopted a little girl. This cute little baby appeared to be several months old. We asked the father how old she was, and he said, "She's a year old." To our surprised reaction, the father said, "The orphanage where we adopted our daughter is a wonderful place, but they are short-staffed, and the babies spend lots of time in their cribs without being held." The good news is that now this little girl has loving parents who will hold her a lot, so she will catch up. That is the power of touch and the problems the lack of it can create.

We never outgrow the need for touch. While we may be fully grown, we still need non-sexual touch, for it is critical to our welfare. Yet how many of you receive non-sexual touch regularly? Oh, you say, "That's no longer necessary." Maybe you're a man and are rather uncomfortable with touch from men, or you're a woman and are also uncomfortable with touch from men. Then there's the possibility that you are just uncomfortable with touch in general. Americans, as a whole, are not nearly as "touchy" as people in other countries. When we visit our relatives in Germany, they usually want to kiss us on the cheeks. We're not used to it. But we might be better off, as individuals and as a culture, if we were more comfortable with non-sexual touch among friends and relatives.

Jesus demonstrated the healing power of touch. In Matthew 8:3, for example, Jesus reached out and touched a man with leprosy, and the man was healed of it. Lepers were not to be touched because they were considered "unclean." How many of you feel that you are somehow "unclean"? You have some kind of history of sin or abuse, and you don't feel worthy of God's love.

God is, in truth, willing to touch you. In Matthew 9:20–22, Jesus is touched by a woman who has had a flow of blood for twelve years. Simply touching the hem of Jesus' garment is enough to heal her. When we seek to touch God and he seeks to touch us, it can be wonderfully healing. When we touch each other in healthy ways, and when a husband and wife touch each other in non-sexual ways, it can be a wonderful experience of God's healing love.

THE SIXTH DESIRE: To Be Chosen

We all desire to be chosen. We desire to be selected by someone to be in a special relationship. This longing starts when we're small and is filled when our parents let us know that they are glad we were born. In school, we long to be chosen for the team or to be asked to play. Later we yearn to be chosen for a date, maybe the prom. In our adult years we love it when we're picked to be in a club or organization or we are chosen for a significant job.

Some people choose to be single and yet desire to be chosen by friends. Some long to be chosen by one other person to be in a marriage covenant. This desire for marriage also means that we want to be the only one chosen. Like one of the old marriage vows says, "*Forsaking all others*, do you take (choose) this woman (or man) to be your lawfully wedded wife (or husband)?"

It is a wonderful experience to be chosen. You feel special and accepted. You feel desired. We've often said that the desire to be chosen is the desire to be desired. In marriage it is the desire to be passionately desired. When you feel chosen, you create messages about yourself that are congruent with God's truth about who you are: you are beautiful, you are special, and you are beloved. When you are not chosen, you create distorted beliefs about yourself that are not consistent with whom God has created you to be: I am not enough, I am not lovable, and I fall short of others. You desire to be chosen for who you are, and yet many of you go to great lengths to be things you are not in order to be chosen.

Think about the fact that most cultures have set standards for what is worth choosing. Even from a young age, we worry about how we look, whether we're tall or short, fat or skinny. We worry about our clothes and whether we are in fashion. We even worry about the cars we drive. Mark sometimes wonders if driving a BMW or Mercedes would make him more choosable!

Having money contributes to whether or not we feel choosable. Wealth, in most cultures, is a sign of desirability. So are certain kinds of status. Being a white-collar worker is better than blue collar—or is it? Being the president of a company certainly means that you are really smart—or does it? Working outside the home is more valued than working inside the home.

Sadly, every culture picks out certain people to be undesirable or outcasts. We start doing this in school. So-and-so is a "nerd" or a "geek" or a "loser." Were any of you born into a "bad" family as opposed to a "good" one? Maybe you were born on the "wrong side of the tracks"? Were you born into ethnic or racial groups that culture decides are not as choosable? Our African American friends tell us that when they were growing up, the shade of their skin was an indication of their desirability. The great strength of America, ideally, is that we are supposed to tolerate or "choose" everyone. But many of us belong to ethnic groups who came to this country and found out that they weren't really wanted.

The Old Testament tells of God's "chosen" people, the Jews. It is full of stories of who God chose to do this or that. He chose Abraham to lead his chosen people. He chose David to be his greatest king. He chose prophets like Isaiah to deliver his message.

Jesus, however, tells us that now God chooses all of us. "Whoever believes in him shall not perish but have eternal life" (John 3:16). We've always liked the stories in the New Testament of who Jesus chooses to talk to. It often is not the "choosable" people. In John 4, for example, Jesus talks to a woman who has three strikes against her: she is a woman, she is a Samaritan, and she is an adulterer. She could have been stoned for her sin, and yet this is who Jesus talks to about salvation.

In the story of the Prodigal Son (Luke 15), Jesus tells us of a son who has rejected his own father. After going off to a foreign land and wasting his inheritance on loose living, he finds himself in a pig pen. For a Jewish man this was about as unchoosable as it got. Yet when he humbles himself and goes home, his father rushes out to meet him. Jesus is telling us that God is like that father. However low we've sunk on the desirability chart, God rushes out to meet us. God chooses us—and loves us.

THE SEVENTH DESIRE: To Be Included

The desire to be included is related to the desire to be chosen. This desire, however, is broader. We desire to be included in fellowship with God and with others. We long to belong. This desire is about community. We long to be a part of something larger than ourselves. It helps us feel that we are not alone and gives us a sense of well-being. This sense of belonging gives us a feeling of needed security. Belonging has all kinds of emotional, physical, and spiritual benefits.

The desire to be included starts with the desire in our soul to belong to a family. How good it feels to know that we are part of something larger than just ourselves, that we have parents and siblings. Families can be extended to include grandparents, uncles and aunts, and cousins. We are a clan. We are, hopefully, proud of our name and our backgrounds. We have family gatherings and reunions to celebrate our belonging. We research our ancestry to see how far back we belong. We trace our roots to the original countries to which we belong.

It is a sad thing when we don't feel that we belong even in our own family. Maybe we feel like the outcast of our family, the black sheep. Some of the people we work with were orphaned or given up for adoption. Hopefully, they were chosen to be included in a loving family. While they feel included at one level, their soul often desires to know where they came from and who they really belong to. Some people because of their experience in their families will choose to be included in new families—churches, clubs, organizations, neighborhoods, recovery communities, or even work communities.

As we grow up, we long to belong to a group of friends. It may be the kids in our neighborhood or school. It may even be the "in" group. Others might not feel included in our "in group," but we act like we don't care because we're in. We belong to lots of things as children—scouts, youth groups, clubs, and teams. We all long to be included in something that helps us feel part of something larger.

This strong desire to belong is even behind the rise of gangs. Because many young men have no father to belong to, they join gangs to give themselves a feeling of belonging, of always having someone to "hang" with. In some neighborhoods, being a gang member is a matter of survival.

In our area of the country there is a rivalry between followers of the Green Bay Packers football team and the Minnesota Vikings football team. The one group of fans wears green and yellow, the other wears purple and gold. The Packers fans wear cheese on their heads (we call them "cheese heads"), and the Vikings fans wear Vikings helmets on their head. Many fans wear the team's jerseys, especially of their favorite player. Why? Because people long to belong and be identified with the team.

Ask yourself how many groups you belong to or long to belong to. Consider your neighborhood or town. Think of all the clubs, organizations, fraternities and sororities, and (of course) churches you might belong to, or wish to join. Have you ever longed to be part of a club that wouldn't admit you? What did that feel like? Do you think that some groups have a higher status than others, and that you've really arrived when you get into the right group?

Some groups can be healthy and fun. Even some that are competitive with each other can create healthy and stimulating activities. Healthy groups—like sororities that sponsor service projects or churches that do missions work—give us opportunities to serve each other. Problems occur when our anxieties take over and we want to make sure that we belong to the "right" group. This is especially damaging when it comes to church, because our anxiety tells us we better be in the right group if we are to be in favor with God. When we're in this anxious frame of mind, we also assume that favor with God will mean that we will get into heaven.

The anxiety-driven need to be in the right group may also tell us that we're in the right country or ethnic group—and that our nationality or ethnic group or racial group is superior to any others. This, simply put, is our desire to be included distorted by the fear that we won't be.

Finally, sometimes our sense of wanting to belong to a group has led us to try to exclude others from that same group. Think of the college freshman who is just dying to get into the top fraternity on campus. After he is invited to join, he wants to preserve his sense that he is special because he is part of such an elite group. So when the next rush season rolls around, he leads the campaign to blackball other students and keep them out.

What have you ever done to get into the right group? Have you ever said yes when you really felt no? Have you ever said you believed something that you did not? Have you ever pretended to be something that you're not? Have you ever excluded someone else from something because you wanted the security of knowing you were right and they were wrong?

God includes us in fellowship with himself and with his Son Jesus through the fellowship of the Holy Spirit. Jesus said, "Whoever does the will of my Father in heaven is my brother and sister and mother" (Matthew 12:50). He also said, "Where two or three come together in my name, there am I with them" (Matthew

18:20). Jesus tells us to include and welcome each other: "Whoever welcomes one of these little children in my name welcomes me; and whoever welcomes me does not welcome me but the one who sent me" (Mark 9:37). The apostle Paul tells us that we all have different talents and gifts but that we are part of the same body and that we belong to each other (Romans 12:5–6).

Universal Desires

Now that you are beginning to understand the seven desires, we hope that you are acquiring a new perspective on the problems you experience in life. They might be your problems or those of others. Underneath every problem there is always an unfulfilled desire. As you begin to understand this, we hope that you will become kinder and more gentle with yourself and kinder and more gentle with others.

It is important to identify those elements at the very depth of our hearts that we all have in common. Regardless of our age, gender, ethnic background, or culture, the seven desires of every heart are universal. When we remember that, we'll be more likely to look for those things in life we share rather than focus on the external problems that divide us. We will know that at the deepest level there are desires that unite us.

We have taught about these seven desires throughout the United States and in a number of other countries. Wherever we go, we find that people understand them and resonate with them. All over the world we have seen people laughing in agreement, nodding their heads, and embracing each other as a result of understanding these desires. For us, sharing these desires with people always helps us feel connected to them. We hope as you read more about the desires, you also will feel more connected with the people you love.

Points to Ponder

❥ As a child, which of your seven desires were fulfilled?

❥ Who helped to fulfill your desires? Mother? Father? Siblings? Other loved ones?

❥ Which desire(s) do you most long to have fulfilled?

❥ Which desires are easiest for you to give to others?

THE PROBLEM IS NOT
THE PROBLEM

Search me, O God, and know my heart;
test me and know my anxious thoughts.
PSALM 139:23

People who come to us for counseling always come with an "identi-fied problem." What we find, however, is that what they describe as the problem is rarely the real problem! We are students of one of the great family therapists of the twentieth century, Virginia Satir. She was fond of saying, "The problem is never the problem."[1] In every case, we can trace the real problem to unmet desires of the heart.

To help you understand how to make this connection, through-out the rest of the book we will be using a model that Satir devel-oped. Many people have used it and adopted and adapted it. It is called the Iceberg Model (see figure 1 on page 44).[2]

An iceberg usually has 10 percent of its mass above the water-line and 90 percent below. Notice that in the diagram, observable problems are the 10 percent that are above the waterline. Now no-tice that at the very bottom of the iceberg is the truth of who all of us are in the sight of God. We are fearfully and wonderfully made

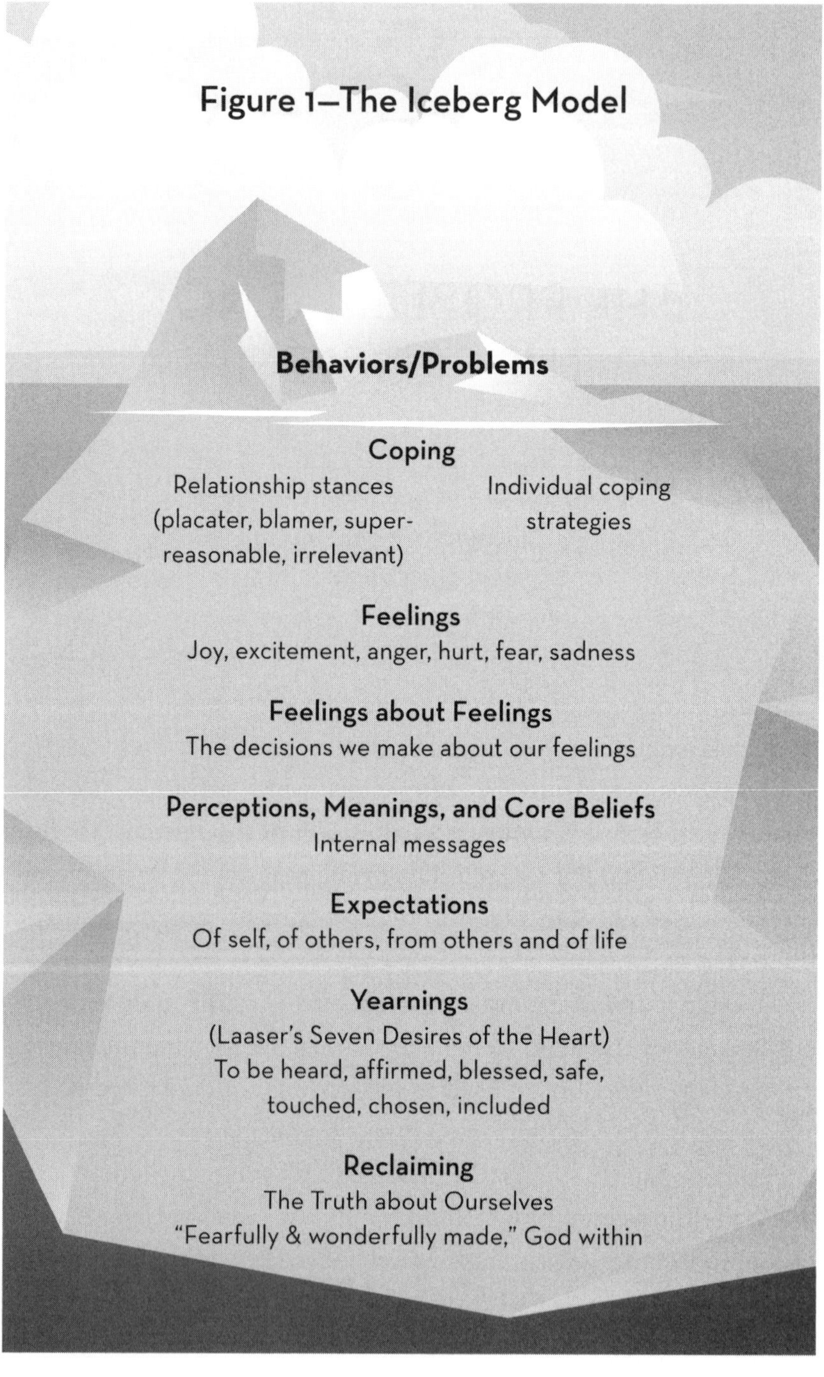

Figure 1—The Iceberg Model

Behaviors/Problems

Coping
Relationship stances (placater, blamer, super-reasonable, irrelevant)

Individual coping strategies

Feelings
Joy, excitement, anger, hurt, fear, sadness

Feelings about Feelings
The decisions we make about our feelings

Perceptions, Meanings, and Core Beliefs
Internal messages

Expectations
Of self, of others, from others and of life

Yearnings
(Laaser's Seven Desires of the Heart)
To be heard, affirmed, blessed, safe, touched, chosen, included

Reclaiming
The Truth about Ourselves
"Fearfully & wonderfully made," God within

and God does love us. Right above that truth are the seven desires of every heart that God put inside of us to connect us to him and to each other. In between the problem at the top and the truth and desires at the bottom are several layers. Each layer describes some aspect of our minds. When we know and understand all of these layers, we will be able to see how the truth about who we really are gets distorted and shows up as observable behaviors. In later chapters we will carefully examine each of these layers and also show you how to make the connections between the surface and the real issues of the heart.

In this chapter we will tell you stories of people who thought they had identified the problem, but really hadn't. They get frustrated when they try to fix the observable problems that aren't really the deepest, core problem. Behavioral solutions to their *observable* problems are only Band-Aids for a much deeper wound. To understand the deeper pain of the heart, they will have to get beyond the observable problem to the real problem.

What usually appear as the identified problems are behaviors that everyone can see and describe. It always seems easier to deal with problems that we can see and describe than it does to deal with problems of the heart. The deeper pain is, well, painful. Most of us don't know how to talk about it because we don't like the pain and we don't have any practice facing it. Besides that, we probably haven't had anyone show us how to talk about the real problems in our lives.

We hope this book can help you begin to identify the deeper pains in your life. When you can finally name your pain, then you can choose to heal the real problem. While it might be tempting to ignore the deep heart pain (and even put this book down!), you will ultimately find that identifying the true source of your problems will lead to a transformed life. The truth of knowing your real pain will allow you to find healing for it at the deepest level of your heart. How else can you truly turn to God for help until you know what is really going on and what he needs to help you with?

When we finally found help for our marriage back in 1987, the problem seemed to be the nature of Mark's sexual sin. When Mark went to his first therapy appointment, he was afraid that the female therapist would be very judgmental of his behaviors. Instead, she looked at him after he had told his story and said, "You must have been in a lot of pain." What a relief that was for Mark!

Don't misunderstand. This therapist didn't let him off the hook. He still needed to find purity, completely confess his sins to Debbie and others, make amends, repent, and make many other changes in his life. Somehow, with all of that, this gentle therapist was able to show him how his sexual behavior was not the core problem; it was, rather, a symptom of the deep pain he had been carrying in his soul since he was a child. Mark had never wanted to accept or deal with the abuse he'd suffered in his childhood, but now with her guidance he started doing so. As he did, he started to heal at the deepest level of the heart.

Following are examples of observable behaviors that really have their root in at least one or more of the seven desires.

Steve and Kathy

Steve was one of five children. He was the third born and as often happens, he got rather lost in the shuffle of a busy family. Early on he tried to talk, but either no one listened or he was told that they would attend to him later. Sometimes others even told him that it was stupid or immature to talk the way he did. In school there were always lots of kids vying for attention. Gradually, Steve became quiet and withdrawn. He had given up on talking. What good did it do anyway?

When Steve was in high school, he began to meet girls. All of them eventually left him because he was so quiet. Then he met Kathy. Kathy came from a family in which everyone talked all the time. The dinner table at night was just bedlam as family members struggled to get a word in edgewise. Many of them, including Kathy, would raise their voice so as to out-talk everyone else. Kathy found Steve to be a refreshing change from what she grew up with. She didn't need to compete because he was so quiet. They dated for two years, and finally Kathy asked Steve, "Do you think we should get married?"

As their marriage developed, Kathy got more and more frustrated with Steve's silence. She grew to believe that she really didn't know him. As she got angry about that, she found herself talking louder and louder just to get some kind of response from him. Steve, on the other hand, responded to her anger by becoming quieter and quieter. The two of them went to several marriage conferences their church sponsored, where they learned some strategies for communication, but they always came away frustrated because it seemed they could never quite get it.

The problem with Steve and Kathy is not really that he is too quiet and that she is too aggressive in her talking. The truth is that they both have deep heart pain about not being *heard and understood*.

Sergio and Leia

Sergio has become a workaholic. He holds down two jobs and when he is not working, he is always busy doing some project at home. His wife, Leia, is discouraged because he is never available to do things with her. She says that the problem in their marriage is his compulsion to work.

Sergio's bosses love him because they know he will always get things done. They affirm him for all the hard work and keep piling it on. Sergio loves the attention that this gives him. When he grew up, no one in his family ever affirmed anything he did. In fact, he was often called a slouch. He got good grades in school, but no one really noticed or encouraged him to go on for college. Now he often feels stuck in his low-paying jobs, and he thinks that if he would just work harder, maybe he could advance.

Sergio is longing to be *affirmed* and to be *blessed*—to know that he is doing work well and that he is worthy. Leia, meanwhile, is longing to be *chosen* and to be *included*.

Juanita and Carlos

Juanita came to therapy complaining that her husband, Carlos, had lost interest in her. She has never been unfaithful to Carlos and loves having sex with him, and is disappointed when he is not interested in her. Juanita's interpretation is that she is getting older and less attractive. She has tried makeup and antiaging creams. She exercises and wears the latest fashions. She buys various sexy underwear and nightgowns, but nothing seems to help.

Juanita was sexually abused by her father as a little girl and grew up assuming that the only way to get touched, at least by a man, was to be sexual with him. As a teenager, she had sex with a number of boys. What Juanita doesn't know is that her real desire is to be touched and held. If she would deal with her old abuse, she might learn that she desires to be loved by her husband with *non-sexual, nurturing touch* just as much as sexual touch.

Juanita's sexual pressure has gradually alienated Carlos. Strangely enough, even though he really likes sex, there are times when he too would simply like to be hugged or touched without having to perform sex.

Lynn

Lynn has a spending problem. Mainly she shops for clothes. She loves bargains and often brings home clothes she doesn't need. Her credit cards are maxed out, and she knows she needs to see a credit counselor.

In addition, Lynn has always obsessed about how she looks. Since she was a girl, she has worried that she isn't attractive, but she believes that at least she can dress like she is. Often she finds that other people's compliments about her wardrobe give her a sense of being special. When other women enter the room, she always checks them out to see how attractive they are and what they are wearing.

Lately, Lynn is wondering if she can afford to have her breasts enlarged. Men, she thinks, really like women who have large breasts. For all her obsession with shopping and with how she looks, what Lynn really desires is to feel *chosen* for who she really is, not for how she looks.

Isaiah

Isaiah's problem, so he thinks, is with fantasy. His sexual fantasies seem to cause him the most problems. They distract him from his work, and he has become more and more bored with his sexual life with his wife. Isaiah finds himself staring at other women all the time. One woman at work has complained to Isaiah's boss that she just feels uncomfortable around him.

To deal with his fantasies, Isaiah prays and reads the Bible. He knows passages like 2 Corinthians 10:5 and knows that he should take every thought captive, but how? Of course he can't talk to other men about these fantasies. What would they think? Christian men don't have these problems!

Isaiah has other fantasies too. In his mind he can be a sports star, a rich man, or some other powerful figure.

Fantasies, like Isaiah's, are one way we can seek to fill the desires of our heart when we feel there is no other way for that to happen. All of the different kinds of fantasy that Isaiah has bring him the desires of his heart. In his fantasies people always *listen and understand* him. There are many *affirmations* in his creative imagination. Because of his success in his fantasies he must be a good man, worthy of *blessing* and praise. Isaiah's fantasies are *safe* because he always imagines the outcome, which is successful. His sexual fantasies bring him *touch*. In whatever Isaiah imagines for himself, he is the one *chosen* above all others, and he is always *included*. Isaiah is seven for seven!

False Solutions and Quick Fixes

When we don't identify the true problems in our lives, we cannot find lasting healing — and when we cannot find lasting healing, we feel lonely, frustrated, angry, and anxious. People cannot find lasting contentment when they seek false solutions to misidentified problems. False solutions are always frustrating and never satisfying, but at least they provide temporary relief. Quick fixes can be more appealing because they do not take time or resources. Yet when we solve only the surface problem, our deeper feelings will always create new problems. For example, we know from our experience in the field of addiction that a person might get sober from alcohol, drugs, eating, or sexual sin, but if he or she doesn't get deeper healing, another problem will surface.

When we learn to identify the real problems in our lives — the fulfillment of our heart's desires — and we can understand how we have missed receiving them in the first place, we can then begin to make choices that will provide healing and contentment. In Jeremiah 29:11 we read, " 'For I know the plans I have for you,' declares the LORD, 'plans to prosper you and not to harm you, plans to give you hope and a future.' " Trusting in God's plan for us, despite how our desires have been neglected or destroyed in our past, will allow him to bring people into our lives today that can serve us with those desires. And when even his people cannot serve us with our desires at times, he will be waiting with his love to remind us he will always be near to hear, hold, affirm, bless, choose, include, and keep us safe.

Points to Ponder

- Think of a current problem in your life. Define it in one sentence.

- Identify the desires that relate to your problem.

- If you are angry with someone, can you identify a desire you are longing for?

- If you are having a conflict with someone, see if you can identify the desires both of you are longing to have fulfilled.

THE TRUTH ABOUT
WHO YOU ARE

People are basic miracles
worthy of love.
VIRGINIA SATIR

At the bottom of the Iceberg Model is the truth about who we are. You were fearfully and wonderfully made, a beloved child of God, made in his image, brought into this world not to be harmed but to prosper. What happened to those truths in your life? The challenge starts, for all of us, early in childhood.

We are born with all seven of the desires deep inside our heart. God puts them there so that we will eventually learn how to seek him to meet those desires. God put them there so that we will relate intimately with others. We are born wanting to be heard and understood, affirmed, blessed, safe, touched in healthy ways, chosen, and included. But all parents are imperfect and the world is not a perfect place. Our desires, therefore, do not always get met. And early in life, we learn how to cope with the fact that they don't get met.

It took our becoming parents to finally get this! We could hardly wait for the day when we would give birth to our first child. We longed to have the opportunity to be parents who would unconditionally love our baby. We would always be patient, always be kind and encouraging, and always give her what she needed—to be heard, affirmed, blessed, kept safe, touched in healthy ways, chosen, and included. We would protect her from any harm, teach her all that she needed to know, and prevent her from stumbling in life. We had hopeful intentions of doing it all—perfectly.

The reality of bringing this precious child into our lives was quite different. Mark was in graduate school, and Debbie was working full-time to support his education. There never seemed to be enough time, money, or sleep to do anything perfectly! And before long, our family grew to include two more children. It became very clear that parenting would become an ongoing challenge to do the best we could. Some days it was better than others. We never lacked love for our three precious children, but we often bumped into our human limitations that prevented us from providing the desires of their hearts.

So what happens to you when you are born into this world, innocent and dependent, waiting for the love and nurturing of others to be safe and to grow with the truths about you? What happens to each of us, born needing to hear *I am beloved, I am lovable, I am adequate, I am uniquely gifted, I am worthy,* and *I have purpose?*

In a perfect world, we would not only be "fearfully and wonderfully made," we would be unconditionally loved through our childhood by parents who had endless patience, resources, and nurturing abilities. We would also grow up in a culture where friends, teachers, church leaders, and the community would treat us fairly, affirm us, include us, and encourage us to be the best person we could be. In a perfect world good things would not change and end, our plans would always work out, everything would be fair, we would not suffer, and everyone would be loving and loyal to us all the time.

The challenge for all of us to find contentment and love begins because our world is not perfect. We live in a fallen world. There are no perfect homes. There are no perfect churches, schools, neighborhoods, or cultures that can give us all that our heart desires. There are many people who do the best they can to be loving, and even then, life is not perfect. In a fallen world, where imperfect people are left to tend to one another, you will get wounded. This is a reality for everyone.

At this point, we would like to stop and ask you to agree to three requests before you read any further. First, please surrender your black-and-white thinking about families. There aren't any totally good or healthy families, and there aren't any totally bad or unhealthy ones either. You don't need to decide whether or not you come from a "dysfunctional" home. We all come from families, and all families make mistakes.

Second, please try not to compare your pain or your wounds to others', especially your spouse's (if you have one). You may have voices inside you like, "My story is not nearly as bad as so-and-so's. Therefore I shouldn't have any problems and probably I don't have much pain." The other side of it might be, "I come from an unbelievably terrible family. How can I ever hope to heal?" Please prayerfully ask those voices to take a rest!

Third, we ask you to set aside any mistakes you might have made as parents. The focus of this chapter is about you and what happened in your life. There will be opportunities as you grow emotionally and spiritually to own, confess, and amend the mistakes you've made. For now, please look at what happened to you.

There are two main ways that people are wounded: The first occurs when something happens to you that shouldn't happen. You were harmed. Boundaries that should have kept you safe were crossed. This is a matter of being invaded.

The second type of wound happens when you don't get your basic needs and desires met. This is a matter of abandonment. Invasion and abandonment can happen to you emotionally, physically, sexually, or spiritually.

Wounded by Invasion

When you were invaded or harmed in life, things happened to you that should not happen. You may have been physically hurt, emotionally wounded, spiritually misguided, or sexually abused. Remembering this harm can stir up feelings of fear, anger, sadness, and anxiety.

If you look at the chart below, you will see general descriptions of how someone can be invaded or abused either emotionally, physically, sexually, or spiritually. Notice that when someone invades you, their boundaries are said to be loose—in other words, they are not in control of their words or behaviors, and you get hurt. When in Galatians 5:22, Paul talks about the fruit of the Spirit and of having such character qualities as "patience, kindness, gentleness and self-control," he is describing a person who has healthy boundaries.

Invasive Behaviors[1]

Emotional	Physical	Sexual	Spiritual
Yelling	Hitting	Teasing about your body	Messages about God that are punitive and angry
Screaming	Slapping	Sexual humor	Self-righteousness
Putdowns	Pushing/Shoving	Sexual misinformation	Negative messages about sex

Emotional	Physical	Sexual	Spiritual
Name calling	Spanking	Touching or penetrating genital area or breasts	Modeling unhealthy lifestyles
Profanity	Watching a caregiver physically hurt someone else (not you)	Being made to watch others being sexual	Black and white messages about faith—no opportunity to ask questions and explore your own spirituality
Mind rape—telling you that your thoughts or feelings are wrong	Restraining you from movement, leaving, or taking care of yourself	Being exposed to pornography	Hypocrisy—caregivers teach spiritual truths but don't exemplify them
Incest—needing a child to take care of an adult's emotions (keep them happy)		Not having privacy for dressing, bathing, using the bathroom	Told not to have needs—that it is selfish
Blaming		Forced to kiss, hug, or touch someone when you do not want to	
Criticizing		Sexual experimentation with other children who are several years older	

Jannea's dad often arrived home drunk after an evening with friends. Her mom fought with her dad and explosively threw lamps or pots and pans to vent her anger. When Jannea came out of her room, frightened and confused, she was told to "get back to bed and be quiet." Although she was never hit, she witnessed a home that was constantly unsafe. She experienced physical invasion.

In Jeremy's home, children were expected to leave their bedroom and bathroom doors open at all times. His parents insisted that there were to be no secrets or misbehaving going on, so they eliminated all privacy in the home. This was a more subtle form of sexual invasion.

When Edgar misbehaved, his mother always asked him, "Would Jesus want you doing that?" Edgar's version of the old song is, "Jesus hates me this I know, for my mother tells me so." The wound is the result of a form of spiritual abuse.

On the athletic field Jane turned her ankle. Her father said to her, "You have to play through the pain." Jane learned to deny her pain from statements like this; the result is a form of emotional abuse.

Alberto's mother was very lonely after his father died. His mother made him the man of the house and turned to him to nurture her in ways that a husband should. When he got married, Alberto had a hard time being totally devoted to his wife as he just couldn't neglect his mother. Alberto suffered from a form of emotional incest.

Mary found her dad's stash of pornography in the closet. As she looked at the pictures of what the women were doing, it imprinted images and ideas in her brain of what women should be like with men. This is a form of sexual abuse.

Many of our clients shared stories about how they were invaded in school. Some were small for their age, or overweight, or slow in academics, or uncoordinated in sports. Some were mocked, some excluded from friendships, and some were hit or hurt because of a characteristic of their body or their speech. Kids can be extremely cruel to each other, and oftentimes, there are no adults who know or who can stop the behaviors. This kind of invasion creates both emotional and sexual pain and wounds in your heart that distort the truths about who you are.

As you think of these few examples and look at the table on pages 56–57, take a few minutes to think about your own life. Then make a chart of your own and list ways that you may have been invaded by your dad, mom, siblings, church, friends, or others.

Ways You Were Invaded in Your Life

	Emotional	Physical	Sexual	Spiritual
Dad				
Mom				
Siblings				
Church				
Friends				
Others				

You will probably not be able to identify all the harm that has happened to you at one time. But you will begin to remember or notice more things once you have committed to this self-examination process. We invite you to become a gentle observer of your life—a reporter of sorts. You are not out to blame those you love, but only to notice things that have impacted your life and will affect what you long for as an adult.

Wounded by Abandonment

When you don't get your basic needs and desires met, you experience abandonment. You can be abandoned either emotionally, physically, sexually, or spiritually. It is much more difficult to look for the ways in which we might have been abandoned, because we don't know what we didn't have if we didn't have it! Life within our own family is what becomes normal or familiar. We don't have expectations for it to be otherwise. Only by talking with others or reading about them can you begin to understand how your life compares to others' lives.

On page 61 is a table of abandonment behaviors. When caregiving adults abandon or neglect the needs of children, often their boundaries are too rigid—in other words, they withhold things that would be good for them to give you.

Just as you did earlier, take a few minutes to think about your own life. Make a chart of your own with these categories: Dad, Mom, Siblings, Church, Friends, and Others. In each category, list any of the ways that you may have been abandoned or neglected. (See table on page 62.)

Ways in which you have been invaded are much easier to describe than ways you have been abandoned. Invasion or abuse involves tangible behaviors that you can see or words that you can hear. If you were hit in the head because you did something wrong,

Abandonment Behaviors[2]

Emotional	Physical	Sexual	Spiritual
Lack of listening (communicating, hearing, and understanding feelings)	Being left alone	Intimacy not modeled	Failure to model healthy spirituality
Lack of caring or nurturing	Being left with neglectful siblings or caregivers	Lack of appropriate sexual information	Lack of spiritual discipline
Lack of affirmation or blessing	Inadequate food, shelter, or clothing, or inadequate medical or dental care	Lack of nonsexual, affectionate touch	No assurance of God's presence, blessing, plan, or purpose for your life
Keeping secrets or telling white lies	Poor modeling of appropriate physical self-care (not okay to have needs)		Left to do life by yourself

the wound is easy to identify. If you were told you will never amount to anything because you failed a test, the harm is easy to see. However, being abandoned or not getting what you need or desire is intangible.

Abandonment and neglect are oftentimes subtle and silent. It can take longer as a "gentle observer" of your own life to notice what is missing. You may never have been affirmed for things you did around the house because it was just expected that you do your part. Or you may have been hushed by adults when you tried to talk about your fear and told that "God does not want you to worry." When you didn't receive appreciation or you did not have someone hear and understand you, it is hard to describe what you really missed.

Ways You Were Abandoned
in Your Life

	Emotional	Physical	Sexual	Spiritual
Dad				
Mom				
Siblings				
Church				
Friends				
Others				

No matter how you were raised, there are positive qualities and negative qualities from every circumstance in your life. If you want to begin the journey of examining your life and understanding how things impacted you, you must be willing to see both sides. Just look at the following two examples.

Anika lived in a totally nurturing and safe home. Her parents took care of all her needs. She never had to worry about anything. They also made most of the tough decisions for her so she didn't have to worry. Today she admits that she has confusion and lack of confidence in making any decisions to take care of herself.

Karl, on the other hand, did not grow up in a safe environment. With both parents working, Karl was left alone with his older siblings much of his young life. His brothers often subjected him to cruel jokes, dangerous tricks, and inadequate care. Because he suffered physical abuse regularly, Karl began to figure out clever ways to protect himself. As an adult, Karl joined the Marines and became a Special Forces officer. His strength and courage enabled him to participate in extremely dangerous missions.

Just as these two examples show, all manner of parenting and nurturing has its strengths and weaknesses. There is no perfect family or perfect community that will provide all that you need. God continues to invite you into his care to depend upon his ability to give you all that you need and desire so that you can live in his truths of who you are.

The Big Deal about Invasion and Abandonment

Being invaded or abandoned has long-term consequences. People who have suffered in these ways usually begin to carry wounds from life. When we talk about wounds, we are referring to beliefs you form about yourself that are not true. Let's see how that works.

When you are small, you are totally dependent on those around you to take care of your every need—feeding you, keeping you clean and safe, nurturing you, and eventually teaching you how to do things for yourself. As long as your needs and desires are attended to, you feel good about yourself.

When parents, siblings, or community are not able to attend to your desires—or when they choose to harm you in some way—you begin to create beliefs about yourself and the world. Since you are young and immature when invasion or abandonment happens, you don't know how to process the experiences in healthy ways. You might even think you are to blame, and you experience shame. You create beliefs about yourself that are not true. Your eyes see the world with a new filter, with biases and faulty perceptions. You make meanings about things you see, and you create assumptions of what others are doing which may be correct, but often are not. And from this place, you wander from God's truth about who you are to newfound beliefs that are not true.

For example, Maria grew up thinking her father did not love her. In actuality, Maria's father was a good man who worked hard to provide for his family. Maria was the fourth child born in eight years to this family, and after her birth, her father began working a second job to make ends meet. Through no fault of her own, Maria did not experience the attention of a loving father—he was absent most of the time. Since her siblings had stories of playing with Dad and sitting on his lap after dinner, Maria decided she must not be as lovable as they. Her belief that she was unlovable was definitely not true, but because her dad was not present in her life, she was wounded, and a false belief was planted in her heart.

Estelle's father was a pastor and believed in giving most of the family money to charity. He believed that it was selfish to provide all of his family's needs because they would not be depending on God if he did. Estelle lived without adequate food, clothing, and school supplies. She began to believe that no one would take care of her needs except herself. As she grew older, she became obsessed with saving—even hoarding—money.

As these stories indicate, from the time you are born, you instinctively long for the filling of the seven desires of the heart, and you expect that they will be given to you from those who love you. When they are not fulfilled, you eventually become disappointed, angry, sad, or anxious. You give up the real truths about who you are—*I am lovable, adequate, unique, gifted, and valuable*—and create new beliefs about yourself and others. These wounds continue to follow you in all your relationships, and you seek others who will either validate your new beliefs or rescue you from them.

If you have a safe place to talk about these beliefs when you are young, you might have a chance to reframe these beliefs. But very few of us live with people who encourage that kind of sharing. Instead, you hide these thoughts away and begin to act out the feelings that accompany your disappointments and false beliefs about yourself.

Points to Ponder

> As you read this chapter, some of your own stories probably came to mind. We trust that God will only allow memories into your mind that you can handle. Pray that whatever you need to heal from will be revealed to you.

> If you haven't done so already, go over the charts and mark down ways you were invaded or abandoned.

> What beliefs about yourself have you created because of that harm or neglect?

> Tell someone you love and trust about your awareness.

EXPECTATIONS:
THE PATHWAY TO ANGER
AND RESENTMENT

*Whoever is adequate? We all create situations which others
can't live up to, then break our hearts at them because they don't.*

Elizabeth Bowen

It was a gorgeous Saturday when Alisha began running through her morning routine of getting three little ones dressed and fed. She also wanted to shower, exercise, make beds, and prepare for a family outing. Ordinarily, these daily tasks would create no emotion — they were her job. But today it was Saturday, and her husband was home, lying on the couch reading the paper with his cup of coffee nearby. Oblivious to the bustling household, he made no offer to help.

By late morning Alisha was extremely angry and made no eye contact with Josiah as she stomped by him, finishing one task after another. They argued the rest of the weekend about how unhelpful Josiah was around the house, creating at best an environment of forced fun for the family. Both Alisha and Josiah were miserable and disappointed that another weekend had been ruined.

At her counseling session, Alisha talked with Debbie about the disappointing weekend. "Have you ever asked Josiah for his help with the kids?" Debbie asked.

Alisha exploded. "Why should I have to ask him for help with the kids? He is their father! He should know that I need help!"

Unexpressed expectations are the pathway to resentment and anger. That is an old slogan of the twelve-step communities. Whether justified or not, having expectations that are not talked about leads to disappointment and distance in relationship. Notice on the Iceberg Model that one level above the seven desires is expectations.

Why Do We Have Expectations?

An expectation is simply an unexpressed need or hope. You have expectations because you are born with needs and desires. In a perfect world, you would not need to ask for anything as a child; loving adults would have taken care of it all. In our imperfect world, your hopes to have all that you need and desire are dashed—and you are left to figure out how you will acquire them in a healthy way. From this place, you begin to develop expectations that other people will be able to help out in your life to give you what you need.

We all have expectations. It is not realistic to think that if we lived a healthy enough life, we could eliminate all of them. Our desires are deep; our needs are realistic; and we do not like to be in pain when we are faced with living without something we need or want. However, we can learn about our expectations and make better decisions about how to deal with them so that our life is more joy-filled.

Expectations in and of themselves are not the problem; the problems start when our expectations are so deep-seated that we cannot articulate them to ourselves, let alone to anyone else. Ultimately, we can use our expectations to enlighten ourselves and those we love about what the deeper yearnings of our heart are and how we have missed getting them met thus far in life.

Why Do Expectations Harm and Disappoint Us?

Why do we even have expectations if they create so much harm and disappointment? What are these expectations and why are they so powerful in our relationships?

To expect is "to anticipate in the mind some occurrence or outcome."[1] It is "to anticipate, look forward to, count on, assume ... require, demand, or insist upon."[2] As we type the definitions, we feel their explosive power! First of all, if you can't externalize your expectations—that is, take them out of your mind and communicate them to someone else—then it is going to be really hard for someone else to figure out what you need and desire.

When you live with unspoken expectations of others, you are like a field seeded with land mines. You ask someone you care about to search through that field and to dismantle those mines, but they have no idea where they are! Figuring out someone's needs or desires without any clues is very frustrating. The person you would like to be helped by is set up for failure, because it is impossible to help and please someone whose needs you don't know. Ultimately, failure to know and communicate your expectations leads to an impasse in your relationships. You become angry or sad, you move away from your loved one, and then you communicate with him or her even less—and the cycle of disappointment, resentment, and anger continues.

If you have not been taught how to talk about your needs and desires, you will continue to look forward to someone else reading your mind so they will give you what you need. You might even tell yourself that if your friend really was a friend, or your spouse really loved you, or your boss thought you were an important asset to the company, he or she would automatically know what you needed. You shouldn't have to voice your need or desire. People who know you well, you tell yourself, should also know from a look on your face, or a sigh, or an overloaded to-do list that you need something! Or if they were really sensitive folks, they should know you need affirming, or including, or touching, or something.

The "shoulds" then turn into blame and demands of others and the world—reversing what *you* need or desire into *someone else's* need or desire to do something about it! Blaming leads others to get defensive and to do and say things that distance them from you, exasperating the whole situation even more. In the end, you get less of what you wanted in the first place. The real disappointment occurs when you give away your ability to do something about your life and trust that someone else will take care of it, for you have then lost the ability to trust yourself to create the life you want.

We already hear you saying, "But why should I get married if I can't have any expectations of my spouse? Or why have friends if we can't expect things from each other?" We want you to know that *having* expectations will be part of any relationship, and that in itself is not a bad thing. What we *do* with our expectations is what gets us into trouble. We want to teach you how to talk about your needs and desires so that at least *some* of the time, your significant relationships can help you fulfill those, and when they can't, you will trust yourself and God to find fulfillment for those they can't.

Why Don't You Just Ask for What You Need?

It seems so simple: if you need or want something, just ask for it. But most of you don't. Why is it so difficult to state your needs or desires? If you examine your past, there are clues that explain how you lost the ability to ask clearly for what you need.

As we suggested in chapter 2, the truth about you included that God is with you and in you, that you are unique, valuable, purpose-filled, precious, capable, and lovable. But since you grew up in an imperfect world with imperfect people entrusted with caring for you, you did not always get what you needed — and sometimes, you got what you did not deserve.

When that abuse or abandonment occurred, you took the truths about who you were and you created false meanings and beliefs about yourself and others. Often, those false beliefs led you to question some of the basic truths about all divinely created human beings: everyone has unique thoughts and opinions, feelings, words, behaviors, and needs. If you are not allowed to have your unique thoughts, feelings, and needs, you will find yourself stuck with false beliefs: *I don't have valuable thoughts, I shouldn't feel, I shouldn't talk, I should do things just to please others, I shouldn't have any needs.*

For example, Sandra grew up in a very religious home and was taught that she was only to think of others, that it was selfish to have needs of her own. As a wife and mother, she did have legitimate needs, but she had been trained not to talk about them. This created a stuck place for her. If she didn't want to be selfish, she had to deny her needs and neglect herself. This eventually led to unexpressed resentment, anger, and depression. Slowly she began losing her desire to live because life felt so oppressive.

Tierra was a beautiful little girl who was included in many of her mother's business appointments. From a very early age, she was told that she was to "be seen, not heard" because these were very important meetings. Tierra loved being with her mom and didn't want to do anything to ruin her chances to spend time with her. But through her years of being hushed, she lost her voice. When she had thoughts or needs of her own, she remembered what she was told—just look good and be quiet. Tierra's distorted belief followed her into her adult life: don't speak up, just focus on your image.

Creating Expectations from Wounds

As these stories illustrate, we can create unrealistic expectations from wounds in our life. For example, if you had a parent who never protected you and who criticized and shamed you, you will long for people in your life who will always be there for you and who will accept you in all circumstances. Your expectations will grow from a deep need to be protected and loved.

If you were exposed to pornography or had other sexual encounters before marriage, you may have expectations for your spouse to perform sexually in ways in which you have been trained. Or if you had an overly controlling mother when you grew up, you may choose a partner or colleague who is very independent and leaves you alone. If you married a very outgoing spouse, you may expect that your spouse will keep your social calendar going and introduce you to friends and colleagues because you aren't good at doing that yourself.

Family, culture, and friends in your past all contribute to how you manage expectations today. When you examine your own life and how you were disappointed, hurt, or unattended to, you can determine what expectations you are creating in your relationships today. These expectations serve to comfort your wounds.

You can also examine what meanings or false beliefs you are carrying from your past that may be affecting your ability to speak up about your needs and desires. If you can't express needs and desires openly with others, then they turn into expectations that may not be fulfilled.

Articulate Your Expectations!

One part of creating a healthier emotional life is articulating your expectations so that others have an opportunity to meet them. Unexpressed expectations often go unmet and lead to resentment. Expressed expectations lead to clarity and trust in yourself, others, and God to fulfill your needs and desires.

Articulating our expectations is risky because once we've shared an expectation with another person, he or she has a choice: to meet our expectation, or not.

We feel best, of course, when our expectation is met—but sometimes other people cannot or will not meet our expectation. When that happens, we sometimes wish we'd never spoken up. But, in fact, articulating an expectation is always freeing, even if the expectation is not met. Only after we have articulated an expectation can we choose to let go of our need or desire.

Mandy always loved having Russ meet her at the front door when she arrived home from work. She expected him to hug and kiss her every day. Russ, on the other hand, was often preoccupied with the kids or making dinner and didn't always think to drop everything to go to the door. Mandy was able to acknowledge her expectation to Russ. Although Russ was still not able to meet her every day, he was able to tell Mandy that when he couldn't, it was not because he didn't love her. Mandy was able to accept and understand that.

How can an articulated but unmet expectation be freeing?

Well, once you've named your expectation, you can begin to trust yourself to find other ways or people to meet your need or desire, or you can decide to just let it go, which is what Mandy did. And, more important, you can ask and trust God to show you how he will meet your desire.

Letting go of something you want is hard to do. Letting go of a desire, indeed, is a courageous act of surrender. When our children were in elementary school and we had to prepare for their school pictures each fall, we always wanted to make sure they looked spectacular. We usually bought a new outfit, went for haircuts, and got up early enough to put it all together. As they grew older and didn't want to look the way we wanted them to look, we realized that we needed to let go of a need we had: to have our kids look appropriate so that people would think we were good parents. Underneath our expectation that they needed to look good was our desire to be affirmed for our parenting and blessed for who we were—regardless of the outward appearance of the children.

Negotiate Your Expectations

Demetrius was a professor, married to a successful business woman. They had two young children. He longed to go back to school to acquire a law degree to further his career possibilities. Both he and his wife had expectations of being present with their children and often leaned on one another when their careers became demanding. If Demetrius went back to school, he and his wife might have to renegotiate their domestic routines. Fortunately, they were able to have conversations about sacrificing time at home if Demetrius enrolled in school. Instead of expecting his wife to figure out how to meet that need if Demetrius was gone, they both made a conscious decision to find other ways for adults to be with their children for the three years of schooling. Demetrius and his wife found other people who could help fulfill their need.

Demetrius and his family were definitely going to pay a price for his further education. Because he was able to talk about his need to be with his children, the decision became a choice, not just an expectation. Choices empower you to take control of your life; unexpressed expectations leave you victimized, hoping for others to take control of your life, as was the case with Andrea.

Find Other Ways to Get Your Needs Met

Andrea, a mom with young children, longed to join the new book club in her neighborhood. But she continued to refuse the invitation of her friends because her husband's work hours varied and she couldn't count on him being home. Her deep desire was to keep her children safe, and she didn't trust strangers to stay with her children. She expected that her husband should be available to be with his children so she could do things she wanted to do. She sacrificed making choices for her desires—being included and having a safe home for the children—and instead, hoped that her husband would change his work hours and encourage her to get out more. She remained disappointed that he often didn't do that.

Eventually, Andrea's friends encouraged her to find other ways to get her needs met. They introduced her to family friends who would sit with her children. And they supported her need to get out of the house and be with other women. It was hard for Andrea to accept that she was valuable enough to use money to spend on sitters and take time away from home when she didn't contribute to the income of their family. It was an old message that kept her stuck without friends.

If you feel stuck, if your life is filled with resentment and anger, look at how you are doing with replacing unexpressed expectations with specific needs. Ask yourself if you can let go of your black-and-white thinking that only one person or one way will work to meet your need. You can get really stuck blaming that one person or that one solution when your need is not met.

You become more resourceful and confident when you have options and choices. You can learn to become resourceful by having several options if you have an important need. When you are resourceful, your anxiety decreases and your confidence increases. "I can do this," you find yourself saying. "I don't have to feel stuck." Trust in yourself grows so you know you'll be okay, regardless of whether others can serve you when you have needs and desires.

Give Your Expectations to God

Emily knew that her husband had been regularly looking at pornography. She had an expectation that her husband would be committed to her sexually in marriage—and fidelity definitely included avoiding pornography. She also had a desire to feel safe and cared for financially since she has given up her career to stay home with the children. While she attempted to make her husband get help and stop his behaviors, he continued looking at pornography. She eventually gave up her efforts to change him and decided that being safe was more important than being chosen in her relationship. It was a sacrifice that led her to great sadness, despair, and depression in years to come.

Emily's story shows us there is one final step in learning about expectations. You may become an expert in asking for what you need, but you still may not get your needs met. What do you do when your plans to have others provide what you need fail? This place is called powerlessness. You can be powerless over getting a need met; you can be powerless over the way you are going about it; you can be powerless over the emotions you have attempting to get a need met; you can be powerless over even having that need. You can be powerless over many things.

When you accept that others may not or cannot give you what you need and you accept your powerlessness in even getting it for yourself, you then grow your trust and confidence in God—the only source of life who can provide. "And my God will meet all your needs according to his glorious riches in Christ Jesus" (Philippians 4:19). God has many ways of meeting your needs. You may pray to him and find that you feel listened to. You may have a deep sense of the affirmation, blessing, and safety he provides.

Remember also that God often works through other people. When you start asking God to meet your needs, you may find that he doesn't always do it in the way you expected. You may think he is going to change someone, like your spouse, your friend, or your boss, so that he or she will meet your need. It may be, however, that someone else comes along to listen or meet one of your desires. Our experience, when we look back over our lives, is that we can see ways in which God brought people into our life to meet our needs in ways we never imagined.

One of our favorite stories of God's surprise provision occurred when we were in a particular time of hardship. Mark had lost his job and was in the hospital. Debbie was home with the three children wondering how to make ends meet. One of our neighbors, a wonderful Christian man, came to the door and said, "I don't know what is going on with you guys, and I don't need to know. What I do know is that in my quiet time this morning I felt God prompting me to give you some money." With that he handed Debbie a check for a large sum of money. We didn't expect that! We had prayed to God that he would somehow meet our needs. Debbie expected Mark to get out of the hospital and find a job. Mark expected that of himself. That eventually did happen, but in the meantime, God brought one person into our lives who made a difference and helped us feel safe.

That is a rather dramatic example. We have many more subtle examples. Perhaps it is a person who at just the right time has a word of affirmation or blessing, a person who just listens without trying to fix, a person who puts a hand on our shoulder in a supportive way, a person who invites us to do something with them at just the right time. Do you have stories like that? Maybe you don't yet, but we encourage you to give your expectations to God and be open to the possibilities of what might happen.

Points to Ponder

❥ What did you learn in your early life about having feelings and needs? Think of the unspoken and spoken messages and the modeling you received.

❥ Think of some situation in your life: when you got married, when you started a new job, when you joined a new church or community, or when you met a new friend. Now think consciously about the expectations you had in those situations.

❥ Think about someone with whom you currently are angry or carry some resentment about. Can you think of some expectation that you had of this person that was violated?

❥ Can you think of a recent example of someone who did listen, affirm, accept you, touch you in a healthy way, did something for you that helped you feel safe, or chose or included you to do something?

PERCEPTIONS, MEANINGS, AND CORE BELIEFS

The roots of all our lives go very, very deep, and we can't
really understand a person unless we have the chance of knowing
who that person has been, and what that person has done
and liked and suffered and believed.

FRED ROGERS

When Erin was a little girl her mom did everything for her. This continued as she grew up even into her young adult years. Whenever Erin would try to do something for herself, her mom would say, "Oh, let me do that." It always seemed helpful at the time. Today, friends of hers are surprised by Erin's passivity. Erin also finds herself getting angry at people when they try to be helpful, and she can't understand it. The worst part is that Erin doubts that she can really do anything by herself. She avoids new ventures and projects. All of this has kept her out of good jobs and also from any meaningful relationships. Erin struggles with some very negative messages about herself and negative meanings she makes about helpful people.

When our desires are not met, we may come to believe certain messages about ourselves. We call these self-perceptions *core beliefs.* It is certainly possible to have positive core beliefs: "I am a good person and God does love me. I am capable—I can do something if I really put my mind to it. I am smart. People like me." However, wounds create negative core beliefs: "I will never get it right. I'm not very smart. I will never get a chance. I am a bad and worthless person. No one loves me as I am. No one takes care of my needs."

Growing up we also learn certain cultural messages about ourselves, others, and the world. These messages foster in us certain perceptions and meanings about life's interactions, conversations, relationships, and events. These perceptions and meanings can be related to gender, race, religious beliefs, age, political feelings, national heritage, and even things like the color of our hair: "All blondes are dumb and all redheads are fiery and temperamental." These cultural beliefs will depend on where we were raised, how old we are, what ethnic background we have, what religious tradition (or lack thereof) our family was a part of, and whether we are male or female.

Core beliefs, perceptions, and meanings are like filters by which we take information into ourselves and interpret what it means. One of Mark's clients was a man who had been very tragically abused as a child. His self-perception was full of shame. One day on his way to his appointment, he stopped at our coffee pot and took out the coffee filter full of used coffee grounds. He showed it to Mark and said, "If you pour the purest of water through this filter, what comes out looks like, tastes like, and smells like coffee. You've been talking to me about the living water of Christ's love for me, but when I pour that living water through the filter that is my brain, it comes out sounding like I am a bad person. Not even Jesus could love me."

Have you ever felt that someone heard you but didn't understand you or get your core beliefs? Perhaps that person heard what you were saying but made a meaning out of it that you didn't intend. Have you ever tried to communicate something to someone else and got really frustrated that they didn't get it? Your interlocutor may have had an emotional reaction, like sadness or anger, that you never intended. Think about times, for example, when you have tried to compliment someone who just couldn't take a compliment: "You say I did a good job, but ..." If a person's core belief is that he never gets anything right, you can tell him that he did a good job but there will always be a *but* ... "You didn't really mean it. It was not that great. You don't understand. There were really problems that you just don't know about."

When we started writing this book together, Deb was trying to show Mark a new feature on a computer writing program. The whole system was rather simple, but Mark was getting extremely frustrated and anxious about it. Those emotions shut him down for a while, and there was no way he was going to learn the program.

This episode had its roots in many places in Mark's childhood. His dad had been impatient with Mark's homework. Many of his grade school teachers seemed to favor the girls over the boys. Finally, Mark's mom distanced herself from helping him with projects. So many years and so many experiences gave meaning to the current episode. Mark's brief reaction was due to old history. When he checked out his perception with Deb, she said she was not angry at all. He was the one who was interpreting it that way. Over the years we have learned to talk about these episodes right away, and that is usually enough to bring our relationship back to reality.

There are so many Alcoholic Anonymous sayings and phrases we are fond of. One that applies here is "stinking thinking." As therapists we're supposed to call it "distorted cognitive reality" or "impaired" thinking, but we like "stinking thinking" better. Here are some one-line examples of stinking thinking:

I never get anything right.

I'm a woman, I just can't do that.

I'm a man, I must not like to talk.

Men (or women) can't be trusted.

You didn't really mean that.

I'm a bad person.

No one takes care of my needs.

If you really knew who I am (my secret), you would not like me and may even leave me.

If I work on him (or her) long enough, I can get them to do what I want.

Americans are good people. Everyone else is not to be trusted.

That religious group (fill in your own beliefs) doesn't know the truth. They might even go straight to hell.

In this chapter we would like to introduce you to some categories that will help you better understand the meanings you make out of life and the core beliefs you carry inside of you about yourself.

Life Experiences

Start with what you learned about your life experience in the first chapters of this book. Do you see how those life experiences shape and mold you? In general terms, your relationship with your father or stepfather, grandfathers, uncles, brothers, male cousins, male friends, and male mentors shapes your view of men. Likewise, your relationship with your mother or stepmother, grandmothers, aunts, sisters, female cousins, female friends, and female mentors shapes your view of women. Maybe they were distant, and you wonder why they didn't seem to love you. Maybe they were over controlling, and you seek to avoid them or you distrust them. Maybe they abused you in some way and they are not safe or trustworthy.

All of us interpret why certain things happen. We wind up thinking things like, "Men don't love me or care about me," or "Women are always busy and don't have time for me," or "Men are not trustworthy," or "I can never do anything to please women." When we grow up, we take these interpretations with us, and we may apply them to men or women in our life, even when they don't deserve them. We make generalizations that simply are not true.

The Larger Culture

The larger culture in which we live and grew up also molds us. We happen to be Baby Boomers who were raised by the Greatest Generation. Our parents survived the Great Depression and endured the deprivations of World War II. They were hard-working people and generally believed that hard work always pays off in success. We were raised in the Midwest with all of its down-to-earth values. Mark primarily grew up in St. Louis and Deb in Chicago. Mark's dad was a minister. Debbie's dad was a mechanical engineer and an executive. Both of our moms were educated and had careers at one time but both ultimately decided to stay home and never worked at those careers again. Our generation of mothers generally thought that women were to work inside the home, and they only ventured outside the home if their husbands were disabled or deceased.

Then, starting in college, we lived through a major cultural shift. America wrestled with civil rights, women's liberation, free love, and America's first lost war in Vietnam. It was a time of unrest, disobedience, and general confusion during which some of the values that our parents raised us with were challenged.

We are two people raised during a certain time and at certain places, and all of those factors influenced how we see ourselves, others, and the world. Take a minute and reflect back on where and when you were raised and what some of the values were of that time and place.

We travel all over the country and the world, and we often are fascinated by the subtle differences even among people our age. One of Mark's German cousins asked him, "How can you eat at McDonald's? Did you not know that they are cutting down the rain forests in Brazil to raise cattle for their beef?" It was not a question that Mark had ever thought about. We often go to Southern California and find a freer and sometimes more relaxed attitude out there. When Mark was in seminary on the East Coast, we were often surprised by their formality. Our Eastern friends always used their good china when we ate with them, while we were more likely to use paper plates. In the South, we find a sense of hospitality and friendliness—even if Southerners are a little suspicious of us "Yankees."

In America we were all taught that America is God's chosen country. Americans generally expect everyone else to speak English even when they are in foreign countries. Our national pride overseas has led to the stereotype that we are "ugly Americans," self-centered, and egotistic. During the Cold War we experienced air raid drills and came to think that Russians are "bad" and Americans are "good." When Mark traveled recently to the Ukraine, he was surprised to find that he actually wondered for a moment if he would be arrested by the KGB. He thought that the people there would all be depressed and angry. In Kiev, he experienced that the people were genuinely friendly and the city was beautiful and, no, he didn't get arrested, although he did walk past the KGB building. Again, we are giving you our impressions of how the time and place in which we were raised affected us. What are yours?

Gender Stereotypes

One way in which our culture deeply shapes our thinking concerns gender — that is, both the culture of the church and broader America culture teaches us certain lessons about masculinity and femininity, about what real men and women should be like.

For example, most men have been taught that sex is their number one need and that it is their wife's job to provide it. Women have also been taught that it is their job to have sex with their husbands often enough to keep him sexually pure. One popular series of recent books even goes so far as to suggest that sex needs to happen at least every seventy-two hours to keep husbands satisfied and faithful. From a biological standpoint, we find that this is just physiologically wrong. We have known countless people who have sex multiple times per day or week, and it is never enough. They will always want more. The brain is such that it will adjust to the brain chemicals that sex creates in it, chemicals like dopamine, serotonin, and adrenaline. The brain will eventually want more of those to achieve the same effect. That is what is called "tolerance" and is a well-known biological fact. Other men are perfectly satisfied with sex once a week.

It is also biologically untrue that sex drive is a purely male phenomenon. We all have been taught that it is men that will want sex and that even when women don't they should give in to this rather insatiable sex drive of their husbands. However, in reality there are many wives who want sex more often than their husbands do, for reasons both biological and emotional. In fact, according to research, one-third of all men are born with low sexual desire.[1]

Another harmful gender stereotype is to insist that a man's greatest need is sex and a woman's greatest need is to talk. In actuality, according to recent research, men spend as much or more time talking than women in any given day.[2]

When we accept male and female stereotypes, we put men and

women in enemy camps. Our jobs become to figure each other out so that we can know how to get what we want. Christian authors would even suggest that it is our sacred duty to serve each other's differences. Deb has found, for example, that many of the women she works with have been taught (again by culture, their mothers, other women, and their reading) that their husband's self-esteem is so fragile that it is their job to praise them enough so that they will start liking themselves.

Men, think about how you teach each other these beliefs going back to your adolescence. Do you really want to be reduced to a set of hormones? Do you really want for your self-esteem to be based on how women treat you? Women, think about how you were taught these values. Do you really want your job in life to be keeping men's self-esteem high and their lives sexually pure? When we adopt these beliefs, they become the core beliefs, meanings, and perceptions that we attach to relationship and marriage.

Our Core Beliefs Affect Everything

Core beliefs, meanings, and perceptions can affect all areas of our lives, work, and relationships. The following are two short illustrations of how distorted core beliefs, meanings, and perceptions can affect relationships.

Carmella grew up in Texas, the daughter of immigrants from Venezuela. Carmella's family was very religious and loved getting together with extended family. In one sense she knew that she was loved and felt very safe in her home. However, when she was a girl, she found out that her father had a long-time mistress. Her father defended himself by saying, "What's the big deal? In our country all men do this." Latino cultures often assume that men have a very hard time being faithful to only one woman, and it is considered macho to have at least one other woman. Carmella's faith told her this thinking was wrong. Now, she finds that she has a very hard time trusting men. The pain of her childhood experience and her cultural learning has given Carmella perceptions and meanings about men that create a filter through which no man can be trusted.

Jinsoo was raised in Korea. His parents still live there. He has come to the United States and has a PhD degree from an American university. He has a very successful life and has recently bought a house. He loves his new surroundings, but he feels guilty because he knows that his parents don't have nearly as much. They are scheduled to visit and he is dreading their reaction to his new house. Even though Jinsoo has adopted American cultural values such as "everyone has the right to own a home," he still has a hard time believing he is worth it. His values and meanings from growing up prevent him from truly enjoying what he has earned. Will he find affirmation and blessing from his parents when they come?

A trustworthy man may long for Carmella to trust him, but she can't. A person might visit Jinsoo and tell him he has a wonderful house, and he feels somewhat guilty.

Core beliefs, meanings, and perceptions are very powerful. They die hard. We once heard someone say that Satan doesn't always have to tell us lies about ourselves, because we do such a good job of telling them to ourselves. Even though we may rationally believe different things today, emotionally the old messages still affect us. That is why there may be those around us who would give us the desires of our heart, but we can't hear or believe that they really mean it.

Working on having greater emotional and spiritual health is about examining the core beliefs, meanings, and perceptions we have to make sure they represent truths today. Understanding the truth will allow us to hear and believe when others are trying to serve the desires of our heart.

Points to Ponder

▶ Can you think of a cultural or family meaning that you learned that you now believe is not true?

▶ Can you think of an example of how someone has said something truthful to you about you that you didn't really believe?

▶ What stereotypes or generalizations did you learn about men, women, sex, money, politics, or religion that you think are not true today? Have a conversation with someone about those and compare notes.

▶ Have you ever had an emotional reaction to something that didn't seem very important? Can you trace it back to some event in your life that was important?

FEELINGS — AND FEELINGS ABOUT FEELINGS

When you're able to identify, feel, and express your feelings,
you can make the appropriate moves, changes, and decisions that
will enable you to experience and enjoy your life to the fullest.
DR. MONA LISA SCHULZ

Most of the people who know Stanley would say that he seems to have no problems. He appears to be content all the time and never seems flustered. His wife, however, has been complaining for years that he never shares his feelings. Stanley is mystified and claims that he really doesn't have any feelings — except for the fact that he is angry at his wife for constantly complaining about it!

When he was young, Stanley's mother had a stroke and became disabled, including an inability to talk. His mother and father lived this way for many years before she eventually died. Stanley watched his father care without complaint for his mother. If ever Stanley tried to explain any of his feelings to his father, his father would remind him that he should be content with what he has and that problems always get better. Stanley learned that it is useless to talk about his feelings and as a result, he stopped acknowledging them.

If you look at the Iceberg Model, you will see "Feelings" and "Feelings about Feelings." We find that most people are not good at *experiencing* their feelings. They may be able to talk about feelings, but they may not be ones that they are really experiencing. Stanley, for example, looked and sounded content, but he was really very angry. He also has a great deal of old sadness about his mother and other issues, but he learned how to deny and avoid that. Desires, Expectations, Core Beliefs, Perceptions, and Meanings create feelings in all of us. You might be feeling lonely, sad, fearful, anxious, angry, or happy (to name a few possibilities), but are you able to experience or talk about those feelings?

Checking In on Your Feelings

We find that men and women alike have difficulty accessing their feelings—this problem is not gender specific, as many books would have you believe. In our counseling center, we often ask our clients to "check in" about how they are feeling. All clients struggle with this one! It is not uncommon to hear, "I need to think about that a little more." Or "I don't know why this is so hard for me." Or "I don't have any idea what I am feeling right now!" Just about all of the people we work with begin counseling rather numb to their feelings. To help them find their feelings, we model feelings to them and present them with lists of feeling words.

It takes practice to think about what you are feeling and to be able to name your feelings. There is a great temptation to use the standard, "I'm good!" or "I'm fine!" or "I'm tired!" So we encourage people to dive deeper into their spirits and identify more specific feelings. (See the Feelings Chart on page 93.) Are you angry, sad, disappointed, hopeful, anxious, grateful, confused, or happy? There are hundreds of emotions to choose from, and just as you expand your ability to communicate by learning more words, you expand your ability to emotionally connect with people when you can more accurately describe what you are feeling.

Feelings Chart

It can help to look at a list of feeling words to help you know what you are feeling. We find that feelings are like the primary colors. There are certain basic ones, and others are mixtures of them. Here is a very partial list to get you started thinking about feelings.

Joy	Sad	Lonely	Angry	Anxious
Happy	Depressed	Isolated	Frustrated	Uptight
Glad	Despairing	Alone	Enraged	Afraid
Enthused	Hopeless	Shame	Outraged	Timid
Excited	Apathetic	Guilt	Hurt	Cautious
Pleased	Worthless	Offended	Resistant	Pessimistic

As you have been reading, you may have identified your desire to be *heard and understood* — one of the seven desires. It is the desire that is unfulfilled in most relationships. "I wish you could really know what I am feeling," says a wife whose husband has just had an affair. "I wish you would understand how hard it is when you don't tell me about our financial situation," says a stay-at-home mom. "I wish you knew why I work all the time," says a husband who feels rejected. If you don't learn how to express your feelings in words and in actions, it is going to be very difficult for others to really *hear and understand* you. They will be left to interpret your behaviors and make assumptions about what they do hear — all of which may be totally inaccurate.

The Ups and Downs of Emotions

If you are going to allow yourself to feel feelings, you will experience the ups and downs of emotions: some will be joyful and some will be joyless. Many people talk about being on a "roller coaster." This is an accurate word picture of how life does seem sometimes. The highs and lows happen when we unleash some of the happy or sad feelings we are holding in our heart.

You may find yourself wanting to rid yourself of some feelings because they are so uncomfortable. People often think uncomfortable feelings—such as sadness, anxiety, anger, and fear—are negative. We don't like using the term "negative" because all feelings are part of us. Attributing positive or negative value to them may cause us to try to get rid of the negative and maintain the positive. Some might think they are more acceptable if they have only positive feelings. They may, therefore, strive to maintain "positive" feelings as their status quo. Generally, we see that many people seek to be happy as much as possible because those feelings are much more comfortable.

When you are faced with danger, it is a good thing that you feel fear and that you do something about it. When you have lost someone or something significant in your life, it is healthy to feel sad and to allow yourself to grieve. When you have been harmed or betrayed in some way, it is natural that you would feel anger. These are all natural, normal emotions that your heart is feeling.

Numbing Our Hearts

As many people grow up, they are encouraged to get rid of the "uncomfortable" feelings in life and to try and live only with the comfortable ones. Thus, we learn to minimize, deny, or cover up feelings like sorrow and frustration. Denial really amounts to isolating or numbing part of our hearts. Gradually, we tuck away more and more of our real desires and feelings. You can see how easy it is to lose your authentic self, to show up in life with only the comfortable parts of who you are or the parts that you think other people are comfortable seeing. In time, you can begin to lose touch with even knowing yourself because you have become an expert at allowing only certain parts of yourself to be expressed. Image management becomes the goal—only allow the "shiny" part of yourself to show up in life, the part that is happy, looks good, and is well-behaved. Unfortunately for all of us, there are other parts because we are human. If we are to accept all of who we are and be known and loved for who we are, we must be willing to be real.

Trying to hide away feelings that need to be expressed is perhaps one of the reasons so many of us are tired. Keeping something under cover reminds us of the Christmases when we kept gifts hidden from our kids because they were supposed to have come from Santa Claus. It took so much more effort to buy them privately, wrap them with different paper and bows than the gifts from Mom and Dad, and then keep them hidden away for weeks so they wouldn't stumble upon them. It was tiring, and we noticed a significant relief when the secret that Santa didn't exist was exposed and we could give and receive in a normal way.

Wouldn't it be a relief if we could just have feelings as they come—talk about them and then make decisions about them without it being a big deal? We believe we spend much effort trying to cover emotions up and portray a perfect life. And it is tiring.

In the Bible all emotions are experienced by the heart: love and hate (Psalm 105:25; 1 Peter 1:22); joy and sorrow (Ecclesiastes 2:10; John 16:6); peace and bitterness (Ezekiel 27:31; Colossians 3:15); courage and fear (Genesis 42:28; Amos 2:16). We need to work on being authentic—knowing what our heart feels so that we look and sound and behave in congruent ways. "I know, my God, that you test the heart and are pleased with integrity" (1 Chronicles 29:17). By training the heart to feel and share emotions, we will eventually learn empathy.

Empathy is the ability "to identify with and understand another's situation, feelings and motives."[1] You feel close to one another when you can share at an emotional level. Feelings are the building blocks of your heart. With your feelings, you are able to connect with yourself and with others emotionally.

Embrace Your Feelings

Stanley, who we described above, continued to go through life emotionless until it was announced in church one Sunday that the wife of one of the older couples in the congregation had recently suffered a stroke. Stanley found the husband during the coffee hour and said how sorry he was for this loss. The husband looked back at him and thanked him for his concern with tears in his eyes. The husband said, "I'm really sad." Stanley went home and told his wife about this brief encounter. When he did, a flood of tears came over him, and his wife hugged him. In a way, Stanley had finally found his feelings. Stanley had embraced his sadness.

We encourage you to embrace your feelings too—to feel the feelings you are having. When you don't, your physical, emotional, and spiritual health is affected. When you embrace your feelings, you accept that your heart is trying to tell you something and that there is something you can learn about yourself. If you keep pushing feelings away—whether it is subconsciously or purposefully—you miss the opportunity to grow and to make a choice about what you want to do about your feelings.

The Physical Consequence
of Unexpressed Feelings

If you choose to ignore your feelings, they *will* go underground and drive your life, whether you like it or not. Physically, this can happen when your body carries the unexpressed feelings you have and expresses them by breaking down in some way. Psychosomatic medicine is the science of studying that phenomenon—how the body, mind, and spirit affect one another. All functions of the body are interrelated, and everything we think, feel, and do is important to the physical health of our whole person. Many times we discount the importance of the feeling part of our bodies.

Think about your own life and the physical pain you have endured. Was there any emotional component that you were also trying to endure, perhaps without much support or much time to fully express your heart? Have you ever been, for example, "uptight"? When that happens your muscles are telling you that your heart feels fear. Have you ever "stomached" a situation? Your intestines are telling you that you are afraid and anxious. Have you ever said to someone, "You give me a real headache?" The muscles in your head or the veins in your brain are telling you that you feel angry. We are not suggesting that all illness is caused by unexpressed feelings, but research supports that much of our physical pain follows emotional pain. The Bible says, "A heart at peace gives life to the body" (Proverbs 14:30).

Debbie experienced a transient ischemic attack (a short-term paralysis) just one month before Mark's addictive behaviors were disclosed. While she had no conscious knowledge of Mark's secret life, she is convinced today that her heart knew about the anguish in her life at an unconscious level.

Mark suffered extreme migraine headaches when he was living a double life. After receiving help and living a life of honesty and integrity, he no longer experiences those headaches.

Jennifer, a client of ours, suffered severe stomachaches while trying to deal with the fear of leaving an unfaithful husband. Samuel was taking anti-anxiety medication and struggling with vertigo until he finally began remembering the sexual abuse in his life. As he counseled, prayed, and began healing from that pain, his symptoms of vertigo and anxiety diminished. We could share hundreds of stories like this of how physical symptoms express emotional feelings.

Living on Autopilot

Your unexpressed emotions can also affect your emotional health—or your ability to make healthy choices for yourself. When you don't allow yourself to feel an emotion, you will live your life on autopilot. This simply means that you will figure out ways to avoid your feelings, and most of the time, you don't even know that is what you are doing.

Margaret was doing very well after her divorce from her verbally abusive spouse. She had spent time grieving her lost marriage, creating safe boundaries, and finding new friends. But her boss had become very critical of her and she didn't know why. She was afraid of him and the possibility of losing her job, but didn't take time to talk to anyone about it or understand her triggers. In the next month, she gained fifteen pounds. She had returned to her pattern of eating when she was anxious.

Every time you avoid feelings, as Margaret did, rather than embrace and attend to them, you disengage from yourself and others. You are on autopilot, and you do things that bring you comfort because they are familiar, not necessarily because they are healthy for you. Watching TV because you're bored, drinking to relax, acting out sexually to feel loved, reading romance novels to feel passion, fantasizing to feel included, or sleeping excessively to avoid something are some of the ways we slip into autopilot and let our choices be determined by unexpressed feelings.

Emotions and Spirituality

You can also suffer spiritually when you ignore your feelings. Since emotions are at the core of who you are—your heart—you miss the possibility of learning what God may want to teach you through discomfort, suffering, or sacrifice. Tim Clinton, a psychologist and the president of the American Association of Christian Counselors, once said, "There are places in the soul that we can only experience through pain."[2] The experience of suffering is profoundly spiritual, for it wakes us up to our dependence on God and our common humanity.

Not only do we suffer spiritually when we ignore our feelings, but we come alive spiritually when we stop numbing parts of our hearts. When we allow all our feelings to express themselves, God is able to communicate with us through the promptings of our heart. As you train yourself to take seriously your heart matters, you will gain a new trust in one of God's most effective ways to talk to you—through your heart. "King Solomon was greater in riches and wisdom than all the other kings of the earth. All the kings of the earth sought audience with Solomon to hear the wisdom God had put in his heart." (2 Chronicles 9:22–23) You have great wisdom from God, too, and training the heart to hear emotions is a powerful way to connect to God.

Feelings about Feelings

Feelings lead to other feelings. For example, when we get sad, we may get angry at the person who caused the pain. "I'm angry that I am sad." Others of us are lonely, and we get sad about that. One of our favorites is that you can get anxious about being anxious.

As we "layer" our feelings, we make decisions about the feelings we are having. I may be angry that I am still sad and therefore,

I have made a decision that it is not okay to be sad. Our decisions about our feelings will come from something we have learned. For instance, we may get angry about being sad because we are taught that to be sad is a sign of weakness and we don't want to appear weak. Or we may get impatient about being confused because we are supposed to know what we want. Feelings are not easy to sort out sometimes, and we can see why so many people would just as soon talk about easier topics. Feelings can be complicated!

The Difficulty about Feelings

The challenge for many of us to talk about our feelings is that we were never encouraged to express our feelings as children. We simply do not know how. If you listen to children, they readily express what they are feeling if they are free to do so: a baby fusses because she is wet and uncomfortable or hungry; an infant screams because he is afraid of the dark; a toddler throws a tantrum because he is angry that he can't have candy; a little boy cries because his friends have been mean to him. Children have lots of feelings and are extremely willing to show and talk about them.

But many families have no patience or tolerance for feelings. We may have been talked out of our feelings, even criticized for having them. Let's face it, it takes time to talk to someone about feelings, and sometimes our parents just didn't have the time or patience to do that. It can be easier to raise children and get things done if feelings are ignored: "I told you to pick up the toys and get in the bathtub." (And I don't really care that you are angry at your sister!) Or, "You have to go to school today because they expect you to be there and I have to go to work." (And I don't have time to talk about whether you are afraid or not.) Do you see how easy it is to create a home where feelings are just not valued?

Teresa said that whenever she had feelings as a girl, her mom would say, "Oh, just think about something else." Or, "Oh, just don't make a big deal about it." Or, "Oh, just don't worry about it." Or, "Oh, just figure out something to do." Her mother was always busy with five children and never wanted to deal with their feelings.

Another reason we may not talk about feelings in our families or culture is that we are not comfortable when painful feelings come up. We don't really know what to do about them, so we brush them aside. "You shouldn't be so sad about your best friend moving away—I'm sure someone else will be your friend. Let's go get some ice cream so you can feel better." Or, "I don't like to hear your angry voice—you go to your room until you can come out and sound more civil." If feelings are pleasant, they are often invited to stay around. But if they are not, many adults will do whatever they can to move them out of the way.

Many people have fear that their feelings will be too painful. They don't want to feel sad, or even mad—they may worry that if they start feeling any of those things, they may never stop. Or they may think that it is "weak" to have such feelings or they will look like a "mess." We can even think that we are going "crazy" when we have painful feelings. We could wind up in a mental institution! Whatever it is, denying feelings will prevent you from experiencing the whole rainbow of emotions, from suffering to joy.

It has been said that the height of one's joy is determined by the depth of one's pain. In addition, growth is inevitably attached to pain and suffering. When you have endured something very difficult —emotionally, spiritually, or physically—you develop a toughness and inner confidence that you can survive and even thrive. And out of that confidence develops a deeper joy for living and a purpose for your life.

Having Your Feelings — The Big Pay-Off

When we allow ourselves to have all of our feelings—to empty out our hearts of the emotions it is carrying—we become softer, gentler people. It is a process of surrendering all of who we are to God to allow him to teach us, comfort us, and lead us to new levels of intimacy with others.

Have you ever poured out your heart to someone because you were so sad? Have you ever allowed someone to hold you when you were so afraid? Have you ever gone to a trusted friend and just vented your rage and anger? Emptying out what is growing in your heart is healthy and healing. It allows those emotions to have a voice and to be heard. Trusted friends may also be a source of helping you unlock and have your feelings. When we say we are with a safe friend, we mean that it is easier for us to take the risk of being honest—to be vulnerable. Friends also encourage us to be honest. Safe friends guard our heart by maintaining confidentiality.

You grow spiritually when you stay connected with your feelings. By staying in tune with your emotions—the essence of your "soul"—you open yourself to God's Spirit and the lessons he may want to teach you through suffering, sacrifice, or pain. James even says that we should "consider it pure joy" when we experience various suffering because it strengthens our faith (James 1:2). When your heart is open and honest, your heart will also receive his love, comfort, and assurance. Do you realize in the Psalms, for example, starting with anger and disappointment with God usually leads to finishing with assurance of God's help?

We want to conclude with a remarkable story from the Bible, about a man who embraced his feelings. Nehemiah, who was a Jewish slave in Persia and who had recently been told of the terrible condition of the city of Jerusalem, writes of his experience with King Artaxerxes and gives us a perfect synopsis of stating his feelings ... and getting his desires met:

> In the month of Nisan in the twentieth year of King Artaxerxes, when wine was brought for him, I took the wine and gave it to the king. I had not been sad in his presence before; so the king asked me, "Why does your face look so sad when you are not ill? This can be nothing but sadness of heart." I was very much afraid, but I said to the king, "May the king live forever! Why should my face not look sad when the city where my fathers are buried lies in ruins, and its gates have been destroyed by fire?" The king said to me, "What is it you want?" ... and I answered the king ... (Nehemiah 2:1–5)

Nehemiah took a chance to be authentic and share his feelings with the king. He could have said a lot of things when the king noticed he looked sad: he could have told a little white lie and said someone had told him something sad; or he could have said, "Nothing is wrong"; or he could have said, "It's really no big deal." But he didn't. He chose to be honest and tell him why his heart ached and was sad. And the beautiful ending was that Nehemiah was given all that he needed to make the trip back to his homeland, and then some. It all became possible because he was courageous enough to answer the king honestly about feeling sad. He had integrity of heart.

The great question for all of us is whether we will have the courage to have integrity of heart so that we may have the opportunity to hear God, connect with ourselves and others, and be served the desires of our heart.

Points to Ponder

❥ Turn to the Feelings Chart on page 93. What are you feeling right now?

❥ Are there certain feelings that you try to hide away or numb? Why?

❥ When you were growing up, were you encouraged or discouraged from having feelings?

COPING INDIVIDUALLY

I do not understand what I do.
For what I want to do I do not do, but what I hate I do.
ROMANS 7:15

We come to the last level of the Iceberg Model that is just below the waterline—it is called "Coping." We cope with our feelings, frustrated expectations, core beliefs, meanings, perceptions, and unfulfilled desires. Unhealthy coping refers to the way we avoid or numb the painful feelings, finding ways to comfort or protect ourselves when we are hurting. Coping can also be a way we attempt to find a solution to the seven desires of our heart.

Unhealthy coping is a false solution in that we hope the coping strategies will work, but they never do. Sometimes these coping strategies can be observed or seen. Sometimes they are internal in the ways we think. We can cope in one of two ways: as individuals and in relationship. We will talk about individual coping in this chapter and coping in relationship in the next.

There are hundreds of possible ways that we cope as individuals. Think back to your own family. What did you observe while growing up about how your family coped with stress, tension, anger, anxiety, or sadness? Mark's family, for example, was one of the first in the neighborhood to own a TV back in the 1950s. On any given day his family would gather around the TV. Rather than talking to each other, they spaced out in front of it. In addition, Mark's dad smoked and loved sports. So Mark grew up in a home that used TV watching, smoking, and sports to numb their pain.

In Debbie's family, she learned to not talk about her feelings. She had a way of withdrawing. Her dad tells the story of how he would sometimes find her under the bed when he came home from work. She even had a stash of cookies under there!

We learn our first coping skill in childhood, but of course, we are exposed to more coping skills as we grow up and venture into the world. For centuries people have coped by drinking or using drugs. Some drink to relax or escape. Others drink because it removes their shyness and it helps them be more social.

Eating is a very common form of coping, as it often represents doing something positive and nurturing. How many of us have a comfort food? What is yours? Some people can be overeaters and others binge eaters. Some people cope with food so much that their eating becomes an eating disorder, such as overeating, binge eating, bulimia, or anorexia.

Today, many people use the Internet to cope with their loneliness, boredom, stress, sadness, anxiety, or anger. Some look at pornography (it is estimated that as many as two-thirds of all Christian men and one-third of all Christian women are involved with Internet pornography). Some shop on the Web. Others gamble. Many get hooked into online games. Some people simply fritter away hours, darting from one website to another.

Perhaps the most socially rewarded way to cope as an individual is to work. If one is lonely, depressed, avoiding tensions at home, angry about a variety of things, anxious about money or social position, there is always work. One can get lots of affirmations for working and it may, but not always, lead to financial reward. It is always a great excuse to say, "Sorry, I've got to go to work. I'm just trying to do well and earn enough money for the family."

In one very informal study that Mark did with twenty-five pastors, he found that almost 90 percent of them reported being workaholics. The pastors were coping with the loneliness of their role, the stress of the demands of the job, low pay, and a variety of tensions at home.

Getting angry can be a form of coping. For one thing, it may be the expression of frustrated desires which are usually not consciously understood. Many families are not good at expressing feelings, except for anger. Possibly one member of the family was allowed to be angry, either mom or dad. No one talked about sadness or anxiety or pain of any kind. Anger then became a way of stirring things up without getting into the pain. A lot of people use anger as a way of avoiding their deeper pain and other feelings. Anger may be expressed toward a relationship that we find unfulfilling. Rather than talk about that, we can get angry at the other person and thereby push them away so as not to have to deal with the deeper issues of disappointment, sadness, or loss.

Withdrawal can be a way of coping, and can take a variety of forms. Reading the paper, watching TV, cleaning all the time, sleeping a lot, talking on the phone to others, and (of course) work can all be ways that we avoid those around us. Isn't it frustrating to have someone close to you just seem to be "gone"? Some of us don't even need an activity. We can use our mind to escape. Mark calls it "going to the land of Numb." It is a special place of fantasy and busy thoughts. Debbie knows when Mark goes there as he can look like he is paying attention to her but he is just not "present."

For those of us raised in religious homes, even faith can be used as a way of avoiding. Our Christian culture is partly to blame for this. Think about being in church and asking someone how they're doing. No one is honest, and perhaps you don't really want them to be. Your question is just a formality. Most of us go to church wanting to impress our pastors and others with how "good" we are. In our services we put on smiles and "raise a joyous song to the Lord," all the time worrying about money, work, the kids, or other tensions at home. In our Protestant churches we don't even confess our sins directly to one another but prefer to do it in silence.

Often we hear religious platitudes that talk us out of our feelings. Mark's dad always quoted Romans 8:28, "In all things God works for the good of those who love him." While we certainly agree with that and know it's true, verses like this can be quoted to avoid talking about any serious issues. If you say that you're worried about money, someone might reply, "Well, you just need to trust God. He always provides." We find that this correct theology is often used to avoid listening to problems we don't want to deal with. We wind up not feeling heard or understood. It would be better to listen for as long as it takes, and then, once a person feels heard, we can offer spiritual help.

At Mark's grandmother's funeral he started to cry when they closed the casket. The very kind and gentle pastor came down to him and said, "You know that your grandmother is in heaven and that you'll see her again. Wouldn't it be better to smile at the knowledge of that?" At that point you don't know whether or not to say "Amen." He knew he would see her again, but hopefully not for at least fifty years. Was it all right to be sad then? We call what happened, "correct theology, incorrectly timed."

When all else fails, one way to cope with our problems is to blame them on others. When Mark was in the fourth grade, he had trouble with his weight and health. He missed a lot of school and wasn't really happy when there, as he was teased a lot. As a result, he got very bad grades. His dad looked at his report card and said, "This is no big deal. Your teacher is the sister of our local Catholic priest." That is all he said, but the implication was clear, "We are

Protestants, she is a Catholic. Catholics don't like us very much, so she gave you bad grades." One innocent woman was blamed, and the result was that no one talked about the feelings Mark was having. How was your family with accepting responsibility for their mistakes? Did they admit them and say they were sorry? Or did they blame someone, including someone else in the family?

Are you beginning to get the idea that there are various ways we can cope with our feelings and hundreds of variations of those ways? Below is a partial list of individual coping strategies:

Coping Strategies

Alcohol	Sarcasm	Gambling	Withdrawing
Illegal Drugs	Sleeping	Internet	Watching TV
Food	Video Games	Nicotine	Busyness
Caffeine	Working	"Fixing" Others	Sports
Shopping	Criticizing	Cleaning	Lying
Preaching	Daydreaming	Exercising	Reading

Of course, not all of those activities are inherently bad. You can certainly read, shop, work, or do anything for healthy reasons, just as you can compulsively turn to them to avoid feelings. You will need to discern when you are choosing to do something because the feelings you are experiencing are too uncomfortable to address. As you work on becoming the person God calls you to be, you may recognize the need to stop certain coping behaviors. This is a matter of emotional and spiritual growth.

Points to Ponder

❧ Make a list of your own coping strategies.

❧ Decide if you would like to change or eliminate any of your coping behaviors.

❧ Would you be willing to admit to someone your need to change?

❧ Would you be willing to ask someone to help you with that?

COPING
IN RELATIONSHIP

For everyone looks out for his own interests,
not those of Jesus Christ.
PHILIPPIANS 2:21

As we discussed in the previous chapter, there are many ways that individuals cope with uncomfortable situations. In this chapter, we want to focus on the ways we cope with our unfulfilled desires in relationships. When we have unfulfilled desires in a relationship, we do things to try to cope with the fear, anger, hurt, or other negative emotions that threaten to boil up. We think that there are four basic strategies for coping with these feelings in relationships. We can illustrate them with what Virginia Satir called "stances." The following illustrations will help you get a picture of what this is about.

The Placater Stance

Someone in the placater stance will do anything to please someone else. When they first see this stance, some feel that it looks like begging. Others call it proposing. It could be that it is begging, pleasing, or pleading. When you look at it, you might like it. This person will do anything to keep the other person in the relationship from being angry or judgmental. The placater is not only worried that the other person will be angry, he or she is also anxious that the other person will leave, perhaps even permanently. He or she buries his or her own needs so as to focus on the other person's needs.

Figure 2 –
The Placater Stance[1]

The Blamer Stance

In the blamer stance, a person sees the faults in others and points them out. A blamer is always judgmental and often angry. See how the hand is on the hip and the finger pointed at the other person's nose? When the placaters see blamers pointing at them in this way, they may continue to placate so as to stop them from being angry, or they may move their up-turned hand so as to ward off the blame. Placaters will also drop their head so that they don't need to

Figure 3 – The Blamer Stance

look at the blame. With their head bowed, the placater looks filled with shame. Blaming and shame usually go together like this.

It could be that when the placater becomes shameful, the blamer will change their approach and come over and pat the placater on the head saying, "Oh, you poor thing. Don't feel so bad." That patronizing reaction is exactly what the placater is hoping for. He or she has succeeded in getting the blamer to stop blaming—but it still does not feel good.

You will notice that it is not a very big shift for the blamer to change their pointing hand into a fist. Although it is far less common, it could be that the anger of the blamer turns to rage and the physical expression of it.

Placaters have two more options. They can stand up and blame back. Now we have two blamers pointing their fingers at one another—this is your typical argument. Placaters can also simply turn their back on the blamer and leave either emotionally or physically.

The Super-Reasonable Stance (The Know-It-All Stance)

Someone in a super-reasonable stance is one who thinks that he or she is right about something and intends to prove to the other person that this is so. Super-reasonable people may think, in general, that they know everything. They are the know-it-all. They look confident, cocky, and perhaps even arrogant. They nod their heads as if they just know they are right. They may look at the other person as if they are really stupid. Super-reasonable people are capable of arguing, but not in a blaming way. They may build a case by citing every example they can think of as to why they're right. Christian super-reasonable people may even quote Scripture to prove they are right.

Often it happens that the other person in the relationship also becomes super-reasonable. Now we have a "reasonable" argument in which someone has to win and someone has to lose. Someone is right and someone is wrong. Someone is "up" and someone is "down." The hope is that there will be a resolution to the problem and then both people can feel good. These arguments are calm and voices are not raised, but no one ultimately feels satisfied as no one is really being heard and understood.

For some, being super-reasonable also means that they are being super-religious. They feel that much of their reasonableness is due to their "true" knowledge of God. They act as if they are religious authorities on everything and every topic. When they "know" they are right, they might quote Scripture, chapter and verse, to prove their points.

In our work with couples who are struggling with sexual brokenness, we frequently run across arguments about the frequency of sex and one partner's availability for it. A super-reasonable per-

Figure 4 – The Super-Reasonable Stance

son will cite research that says how often the "average" couple has intercourse. He or she may talk medically about how it's good for prostate health in men or the regulation of hormones in women (all true). Men may talk about how they need sexual frequency to stay sexually pure (not true). When it comes to this argument, the super-religious will quote Scripture about "submission" (Ephesians 5) or the body belonging to each other (1 Corinthians 7). People who argue this way take these passages out of context and neglect the full context of the chapters in which self-sacrifice is encouraged (Ephesians 5:1–3).

The real problem with trying to win an argument by being super-reasonable is that you do not really hear the heart of the person you are trying to convince, and thus the possibility of connecting in an emotional way is lost. Super-reasonable people do not share their emotions in a conversation; they only talk from their analytical or intellectual place. If the desire of your heart is to be heard and understood and to connect emotionally, you must talk about your emotions!

The Irrelevant Stance

Whether they are being blamed or argued with, when someone takes an irrelevant stance, he or she is really saying that they don't care, or that they give up. They put their arms out to the side and just say to the other person, "Whatever!" People who are in the irrelevant stance may do what they need to do to get away when they give up like this. They might actually physically leave, or they might leave in their mind. Whichever the case, they are "gone."

The irrelevant stance is usually one that is taken when people are tired and frustrated. They will say things like "I've talked to you until I'm blue in the face. You just don't understand" or "I give up. I'm so tired of this argument. Have it your way. I'm done!"

Each of the stances may reflect that a person is experiencing unfulfilled desires. Placaters want to feel heard and understood. They also want to feel safe that the other person won't leave or be angry. They desire to be affirmed and blessed and to be chosen and included in the other person's life. Placaters would also like to be touched as a form of assurance that everything is okay.

Blamers know that their desires haven't been met. They have many expectations of others. If they don't feel heard or understood they will say things like, "You never listen. You don't get it. You're so dumb!" If they don't feel affirmed or blessed, their blaming will often express their exasperation about never "being appreciated." If they desire safety, they may be critical in areas where they want help: "You never balance the checkbook" or "You need to make more money." It is easy to identify blamers because their statements usually start with "you." There are lots of possibilities like, "you need to slow down, you need to be more careful, you need to get going, and you need to stop doing that." When they need healthy touch, but feel they are only getting sexual touch, they will

Figure 5 – The Irrelevant Stance

116

blame about sex: "You don't love me for who I am; all you ever care about is sex." Finally, when blamers don't get included or chosen, they are quick to point out how left out they are, or be critical of how much time other people are spending on other activities. They interpret that other people just don't care.

A person in the super-reasonable or super-religious stance lives so much in their mind that they don't have much awareness that they have feelings, much less desires. They are hyper-concerned about being heard and understood. But they will only feel heard and understood if you agree with them. When you agree with them, they interpret that as being affirmed. To them, being smart is the way they are worthy of the blessing. In many ways the super-reasonable person wants to be chosen and included. They deserve to be, so they think, because they are so smart or so religious.

Remember, the person in the irrelevant stance has desires but has generally given up and acts as if they don't care. They pretend to be self-sufficient, all the while feeling desperately lonely about their unfulfilled desires. If they can't win the conversation, they turn instead to taking care of their own needs and become self-sufficient. The irrelevant stance will generally turn a person to individual coping. They have given up on others, at least for the time being. Their core belief is, "No one will take care of me but me."

The Purpose of Stances

We get into the coping stances in relationships in an effort to communicate and be heard by one another. We have desires we long to have met, and we desperately want someone to know. Quickly we discern that our desire is not going to be met, and so we get defensive and shift into one of the stances to protect ourselves from the feelings that are coming. Again, just like individual coping, stances provide us with a way to manage our feelings when we do not have a healthier option.

Alma was really sad as she observed her son's constant use of the computer to play video games. It reminded her of her husband and her father who cope with life by watching too much TV. The concern about the computer use is valid, but Alma doesn't like her sadness. Rather than tell her son how sad she is and talk to him in a healthy way, she finds herself repeatedly blaming him for a variety of things. He doesn't pick up his room, doesn't do his homework, and never seems to have any time for the family.

When Alma's husband, Rick, sees this, he gets anxious because what Alma is doing reminds him of his mother's constant criticism of him. Rick doesn't like his anxiety and rather than share his concerns with Alma, he becomes a placater seeking to please Alma in some way so that she will stop being so critical. When Alma sees this placating behavior, she becomes reasonable with Rick and seeks to explain or defend her reasons for doing so.

Their son, Barry, takes a typical teenage response and whenever his mother criticizes him says, "Whatever." Barry continues to find more ways to play his games in secret.

All three people in this story long to be heard and understood, affirmed, blessed, and safe. None of them has decided to understand their triggers or the way in relationship that they cope. They will never find the answers to the desires because they haven't learned the skills to deal with them.

The Congruent Stance

When we work with people, we show them the stances and have them role-play them. Most of the time, they will instantly identify with one or more of them. At the end of this demonstration we always help them get into a different stance that we call "congruent."

Congruence, in this demonstration, will reflect the truth of who they are in Christ. We have them put their hands at their side, standing up straight. We then ask them to take several deep breaths so as to relax. If they feel comfortable, they will often close their eyes as we remind them of the truth. "You are fearfully and wonderfully made. You are God's chosen child. You are blessed. You are included in God's kingdom. You are safe. You are forgiven. God knows the desires of your heart. Try to focus on these truths."

When we do this demonstration with couples, it is amazing how almost every one of them winds up embracing. Many people tear up as they are relieved and inspired by remembering the truth. We then ask them how they would face any problem in their lives if they were able to be this congruent.

Stances are a big deal. We all use them. We all began seeing them as children and grew up with parents who played various

Figure 6 — The Congruent Stance

ones. Our approach to life may be greatly determined by the stances we have been accustomed to. Becoming congruent will take practice. It is, however, the only one in which we can hope to have intimate relationships with others and with God.

Unhealthy coping, either individually or in relationship, robs us of our true self. It helps us to hide from the world, and we will never be truly known. It is important to know what can get us to these unhealthy behaviors. In the next chapter we want to teach you how you might get "triggered" into your coping behaviors by your interaction with the world.

Points to Ponder

‣ Think about people in your life that you really care about like your spouse, mother, father, friend, or sibling, and ask yourself what stance you play most often with them.

‣ Which one do they most often play with you?

‣ Try practicing with a friend or your spouse all of the stances, including the congruent stance.

TRIGGERS
AND LAND MINES

The art of living lies less in eliminating
our troubles than in growing with them.
BERNARD M. BARUCH

Jack goes to his boss, a man he respects, about a problem he is having. When Jack enters his office, his boss says, "Not now, Jack; I'm too busy." Jack is crushed. Back in his own office, he almost starts crying but quickly pulls himself together. Later, Jack wonders, "What in the world happened there?"

One afternoon, Sonya asks her nine-year-old daughter Samantha how her day at school went. Samantha tells her about several boys who teased her. Not particularly bothered about it, Samantha goes up to her room to play. Sonya, however, is furious. She calls the school and demands to talk to her daughter's teacher. She yells, "I want those boys expelled!"

Mario and his wife Rosie are talking about a project around the house they need to get done. Rosie suggests several things that he needs to do. While she is saying this rather matter-of-factly, Mario hears it as being really angry and says, "Why are you so angry with me?"

Gisela opens the mail to find a "Not Sufficient Funds" notice from their bank. She is horrified, thinking that their financial condition is totally out-of-control. She immediately calls her husband and starts yelling at him for being so irresponsible. She hates herself for being so dramatic, but her fear and anger dictate her response.

These are a few examples of how people get "triggered." Triggers happen when some event in the present takes us back in our memories, some that we consciously know and some that we don't, to painful events in the past. The result is that the reaction to present events seems inappropriate and overreactive. Others will wonder why we are reacting the way we are. In some cases, the reaction leads to difficulty in relationships and in coping with life.

Jack's father rarely had time for him and never affirmed or blessed him. Sonya was teased regularly by boys when she was a girl. For Mario, his mother was usually angry and critical of him and told him constantly that he never did anything right. And Gisela grew up in a family where financial responsibility was equated with being a good person, so any perceived financial failure created feelings of inadequacy.

Our brains store information in a variety of ways. We have two kinds of memory. One is visual. We can "see" events of the past. Perhaps these visual memories are not always accurate, but still we get an image in our brains. The other kind of memory is sensory and emotional. Our bodies store every physical experience we have ever had; how we were touched, smells, voices, and sounds, and even the taste of something. For example, if we asked you to remember the taste of your favorite dessert, your body memory would bring it back to you. Can you remember the physical sensation of your first kiss or the hug of a person close to you? What about the smell of popcorn at the movies or hot dogs at the ball game?

Our brain also stores all the emotional feelings we have ever had. They can get triggered fifty or more years later and still be as fresh as the day they first happened. For example, Trevor was an exceptional basketball player when he was in high school. When he didn't grow in height his junior year, he was cut from the team. It was a devastating year for him. Now a father, Trevor gets extremely angry when his ten-year-old son is not chosen for one of the traveling basketball teams. This incident has triggered Trevor back to the emotions of his own high school experience.

Memory is a very good thing, reminding us of many important things that are a part of our lives. It allows us to retain knowledge and information, which sustains our work and our relationships. Our memories can bring us joy and happiness. Memory also protects us. We smell smoke and it reminds us to avoid a fire. We're near a hot stove and remember that to touch it would bring a painful burn. We hear someone call for help and we know we need to respond. God has built memory into our brains so that we can survive. All of our life experiences build an archive of memories in the cells of our brains, and we can use that information to do great things.

When memories tell us that something is dangerous, we may want to avoid it and perhaps run away, or we may want to deal with it and perhaps even fight against it. This is generally referred to as the "fight or flight" response. It is also called *the stress response.* It is the way we survive, and our memory is a big part of it. Can you remember a loud warning or spanking when you were tempted to go play in the street? Today when you look left and right, don't you have the voice of your parents in your head? Think of all of the experiences you have on a daily basis which bring up memories of the past with various emotions attached to them.

The problem with stress is that stimuli in the present that aren't really dangerous may remind us of danger in the past that was. We all remember the trauma that we as a nation experienced during the tragedy of 9/11. Can you remember the first time you flew on a plane after that? Were you a little more anxious? Did you look around to see if there was anyone suspicious on the plane? We had a major bridge collapse in Minneapolis. For a short while after that, we were unusually aware of every bridge we crossed by car.

Those are fairly recent events in our lives, but sometimes we respond similarly to events that happened decades ago. Since Mark was sexually abused by a man when he was a boy, he still reacts to touch by a man and has to remind himself that today he is safe. The aftershocks of traumatic events can be long-lasting.

Have you ever felt anxious or afraid and just couldn't figure out why you felt that way when nothing in the present seemed to warrant the feeling? Since our bodies store the memories of all experiences, they might "tell" us about pain from the past even if we don't consciously remember it. Headaches, backaches, stomachaches, and pain in all parts of our body might be indications of the stress we carry there. We can choose to listen to these symptoms and ask ourselves if there is something painful from the past that is causing it.

One woman told us that when she needs to make a presentation she gets a stomachache. In grade school, she had given a talk where all the students laughed at her. Afterwards she went into the bathroom and vomited because she was so embarrassed. Her stomach and that early experience stored the memory. Every time she anticipates speaking in some public situation, her stomach reminds her of that earlier event.

When our memories store emotional experiences from our past, we may think that we have gotten over an experience, but our emotional memory hasn't and we still get triggered. Anxiety, loneliness, fear, anger, and sadness (to name a few primary feelings) can be stored for years in our memory.

At a recent conference we attended a dinner. When we walked

into the banquet hall, we realized there were no assigned seats. Even though we are fully grown adults, for just a moment we were back in school on the first day wondering where we were going to sit in the lunchroom. The dinner experience didn't last long as we quickly saw friends and sat down with them. That is not a big deal, but it is an example of how even the most basic of events trigger us into the past.

There is nothing quite like loss to trigger us into painful emotions. One day in March, Mark was noticing that he was feeling sad and slightly depressed. He had no current reason to feel that way. Deb reminded him that it was the anniversary of the death of his dad. For those of us who have lost loved ones, the same time of year can remind us of a difficult time much earlier. The season, the temperatures, and the events of that time of year can be triggers taking us back to that same time of year when we lost someone.

Think back to the losses of loved ones that you have experienced. Do they not still bring some feelings of sadness when you think of them? If you shared a favorite song or food and you hear that song or eat that food today, does that bring back your feelings of sadness? Your memories will make these associations forever.

One of the people we work with recently told us, "My mind has many hurtful memories of my dad criticizing me." Her father was often distant and rarely affirmed or blessed her. Today when she is trying to build deeper intimacy with her husband, this woman has a hard time believing that he truly cares. No matter what he says, the sound of a male voice is enough to trigger her into her sadness and loneliness going back to her dad.

Healing Your Memories

What memories have been coming up for you as you read this chapter? We encourage you to write or journal about them. At the very least, you might think about talking to your spouse or a friend about them. There is nothing quite like companionship to bring us comfort. It is very connecting to share with someone your triggers and the experiences that are attached to them. While your feelings may not go away in the sharing, emotional intimacy is experienced in the sharing of these events. You can feel closer to another person by being vulnerable in this way.

There is a really important reason for doing the work of healing your memories. When we heal memories, we look at the beliefs we took in at the time and reframe them into truths for today. Often our memories affect our current feelings and relationships. If we don't know how to deal with our memories, it might cause us to struggle with feelings and relationships, including our marriages.

Isaac is a very good man, but he struggles with depression. He loses work time because there are days when he can't even go to work. His wife has exhausted herself trying to encourage him. He has been to doctors who have put him on antidepressants, but they don't work for long. What Isaac has never taken seriously is that his father died when he was three, and his mother worked very hard to support the family and was hardly ever home. Isaac had to fend for himself with little support or encouragement. He has been sad and lonely all his life, and the feeling of sadness has become a rather familiar way he handles life. Now this sadness is affecting his work and his marriage.

Julianna grew up with a mother who struggled with anxiety. Her mother's anxiety expressed itself in the constant questions that she asked. Juliana learned to answer them quickly and to shut down from talking to her mom. Every time Julianna had some-thing to say or ask, her mother had many questions. She learned to be anxious too—would there be more questions? Now that she is married, she finds that there are times when her husband asks her a question, and it causes her to want to shut down and avoid him.

Needless to say, this is having a very negative effect on him, as he has begun to think that she doesn't really care.

Neither Isaac nor Julianna grew up with affirmations or blessing. In some ways they also didn't feel safe. Today the emotions they carry from the past continue to cause them difficulty. It is hard to affirm or bless someone who carries such feelings, as they will discount those messages.

How the Desires Are Triggered

More than likely, one of your seven desires was not met when you were a child. Now, in your adult life, seemingly innocent situations will trigger that desire in powerful and complex ways.

Those who weren't heard or understood growing up may struggle to find their voice — to be able to speak about what they feel, need, or desire. Or they may talk a lot. Anyone who doesn't seem to listen or understand can take them back to the past hurt they've known. Their resulting anger or sadness can in fact work against them because it pushes people away.

Those who didn't get affirmed struggle to know if they ever got things right. Any criticism, however constructive, might take them right back to their guilt and feelings of always being wrong. Someone who doesn't say, "Thank you!" may create anger or drive them into thinking, "I probably didn't get it right." Even if given a compliment, they might not believe it.

The lack of blessing causes shame and a constant need to find blessing. Those who were never blessed will constantly need approval, but it never seems to accomplish the desired result. Anyone around them may be put off by their self-centeredness, and the resulting complaints will take them right back to their painful emotions.

Growing up with a lack of safety creates feelings of fear and anxiety. In the present, people who suffer with these feelings will get triggered by any perception on their part that things are not safe. Perception is the key. You can perceive that something is dangerous even when it is not. Remember Mark's example: a man touching him today is really not dangerous, but the touch takes him back to times when that touch wasn't safe.

Lack of healthy touch leaves a chronic touch deprivation. When people long deprived of touch relate to others who don't touch, they will feel unloved and unsupported. They may turn to sexual ways of getting touched, getting them into real trouble. When a spouse says no to sex, these people get triggered to deep levels of abandonment and may react in ways that completely shock their partner.

Not being chosen leaves wounds of feeling unattractive and unlikable. People with such wounds constantly compare themselves to others. Anyone who they perceive looks or acts better or who has achieved successful things may trigger them into feeling totally unworthy. A friend or spouse may tell them they look good, but they don't believe it.

Those who were not included as children may spend their adult lives either constantly striving to fit in or avoiding social situations altogether. The sense that they haven't been invited or included will trigger feelings of pain. The people who strive to fit in will say yes when they mean no, and will act in certain ways so as to be a part of the group. They will then be chronically disappointed in themselves and feel even more left out. Those who avoid social situations will not even attempt to fit in. They stay quiet, alone, at home, and rarely venture out.

Some people will try to eliminate triggers in their lives because triggers create emotional pain. Any of the coping strategies that we talked about in chapter 7 can be used to escape or medicate the pain. But these coping strategies are, at best, quick fixes and distractions — none of them creates long-term healing.

So what does? The ultimate goal is to be able to name the trigger, to trace it back to its origin, and then to make a choice about it in the present. It is not possible to eliminate triggers if you are going to be in relationship with others. When we live life in relationship, we will be triggered. And emotionally healthy people will recognize that the person who triggered your intense feelings did not intend to hurt you.

We would like to share a recent example. It was nearly Thanksgiving as we were finishing up these chapters, and we had been traveling for several weeks for speaking events. Life was too busy, and Debbie had numerous things to do to prepare for our out-of-town trip to be with family. Fatigued, Debbie found herself withdrawing and making sarcastic remarks to Mark when he was asking simple questions. These coping behaviors were all about Debbie being overstressed. So while he did not appreciate her snapping remarks, nor her pulling away, he did not assume that *he* was the problem or that she did not care about him. Fortunately, Mark chose not to fight back even though he may have been triggered, nor did he respond with his own coping — he knew that Debbie's behaviors were not about *him*.

Triggers Can Incite a Vicious Cycle

Triggers can become a vicious cycle when someone who is triggered and uses their coping behavior then triggers someone else. When Debbie gets triggered into some of her painful memories of not being chosen or included, she can cope by withdrawing. Seeing her cope this way can trigger Mark, as it reminds him of the pain of his mother's emotional absence in his life. He then copes by asking lots of questions, getting super reasonable or religious, and this therapist approach of his can trigger Debbie even more. She then withdraws more and Mark gets triggered more. At that point we are "off to the races," so to speak. Sometimes we have stayed in that cycle for days and weeks.

The only way to break out of such a cycle is to begin to be honest about what you are feeling and to acknowledge how you are coping. You can then talk about any of the "under the water" levels of the Iceberg Model—what meanings you are making, what distorted beliefs you have taken in, what unspoken expectations you have, what you need or desire. This is congruent with being triggered, and it is letting the person that triggered you know more genuinely what you are thinking and feeling. This is intimacy.

Another strategy is to take a time-out and really work hard on not personalizing the trigger. You may walk around the block, journal, or call a friend who is able to listen. By doing so, you give your rational brain enough time to override your emotional brain so that you can replace old coping with a healthier choice.

If someone is triggered by you and is using hurtful coping stances or behaviors, it is important not to become a Placater to keep the peace so their trigger will go away. Many of us do this because we are uncomfortable with the painful feelings that surface with triggers. But when we do just try and please a triggered person, we are really enabling the unhealthy cycle of coping. Authenticity is not encouraged, but covered up. And intimacy is sacrificed because neither person has shared honest feelings and, therefore, has not been heard and understood.

As you get emotionally healthier, you will learn to recognize and come back from your triggers more quickly. You may decide to talk about your triggers with someone who is a good listener. Good listeners are those who don't try and talk you out of your feelings. They also do not judge you, nor do they try and fix your feelings or your situation.

Working on having greater emotional health is about examining the perceptions, meanings, and distorted core beliefs we have to evaluate whether or not they represent truths today. In the next chapter we will give you more strategies for dealing with triggers.

Points to Ponder

▶ Think of a recent life event when you were triggered into great sadness, anger, or fear and how those feelings felt out of proportion to the event.

▶ How did you cope (respond) when you were triggered?

▶ Does the trigger bring up painful memories or losses in your life?

▶ Can you relate your trigger to one of the seven desires that wasn't being met?

▶ Remember to be gentle with yourself, because doing this kind of reflection takes a lot of practice.

TRIGGERS AS
TRANSFORMATIONS

Do not conform any longer to the pattern of this world,
but be transformed by the renewing of your mind.
ROMANS 12:2

Rachael was sexually abused as a young teen. As a result, she had trouble being sexual when she married. Once she realized that sex triggered her into the pain of the abuse, she decided to tell her husband about the past abuse. He completely understood and became her companion in the pain. He helped her to heal by not being aggressive about sex and never demanding it. In so doing, he helped her to heal by finding out that he could be safe.

Triggers can be painful and lead us to all sorts of problems. We'd very much like to have them go away, to be rid of them. So, you ask the question, "How can we heal from all of these triggers?" People of faith hope that they can be healed or "delivered" from triggers. We might pray, "God take the pain away." When God doesn't seem to heal the pain, we can become disappointed and angry. The problem is that triggers come out of our memory, and our memory is not going away. We really don't want our memories to go away; they are a part of the way we survive. So what do we do?

When triggers happen we need to make healthy choices about how to deal with them. At that point we can turn triggers into moments that transform our lives. Triggers can become transformations.

As we have grown in our faith and in our healing, we no longer fear getting triggered. Our triggers used to cause us pain for days; now we deal with those triggers in minutes or hours. As we grew in our faith and maturity, we learned how to process the triggers and find deeper answers and meaning in them.

Owning Our Own Triggers

When we get triggered, our first and biggest temptation is to blame whatever person or stimulus we think caused us to be triggered. We might say that "My spouse just doesn't get it" or "My boss is really cruel" or "The weather is so bad, I'm so depressed." In the worst case spiritually, we might even blame God.

There are, of course, times when someone is really doing something to hurt us in the present. In those times our emotional reaction may be very current and appropriate to the event. There are also times when catastrophic events happen that are out of our control and we are triggered. There are times when God does not seem to intervene to stop painful events or losses. We might need to confront the hurt or use healthy coping to deal with the pain of it. Even when our triggers are current and real, we are responsible for how we react to these issues.

Remember that we filter all information coming into us. Our filter is based on our life experience, our core beliefs, our meanings, and our perceptions. All of those are based on how we were raised and in what culture and time we grew up. We all can react differently to the very same person, event, or stimulus. This is based on how the new information gets processed by our memories. What experiences in the past does the new trigger tap into? So, as you now know, your physical and emotional reactions may largely depend on how you learned to deal with experiences rooted in your childhood.

It is helpful to learn that just because you are triggered by a situation, someone else may face the same situation and not be triggered at all.

Maria came from a lively Italian family who engaged in loud, aggressive conversations. She married William, who was an only child and whose family was very quiet. They never debated any subject nor tolerated rambunctious voices. One day a neighbor stopped by to loudly complain about the barking dogs across the street. Maria chuckled and agreed that the dog was a problem. William, on the other hand, felt attacked and retreated into the house.

Here is one situation, experienced by two people with two very different reactions. These two people had very different life experiences through which to filter a current situation.

When we accept that we possess a filter unique to us, we are on the journey to "own our own triggers." We know that our reactions belong to us and not to others. This is an important step of maturity. It allows us to stop blaming and to start growing. Rather than saying, "You did this," we say, "I can see how I reacted to this and where my trigger comes from." We start remembering stories of our past and realize how strong the feelings are that we bring into the present. If we are really growing and maturing, we also talk to others about our history and reactions. We process what is happening to us and we get feedback on how we perceive our reactions. Close friends, family, spouses, pastors, or counselors can help us discover and deal with our triggers. If we can find safe people, they may even be able to talk us through the trigger, helping us to interpret it, and encouraging us to make healthy choices about it.

Roy grew extremely angry about a sermon his pastor gave about God's providential care. He began by complaining to many around him about how inconsiderate and stupid the pastor was. But then Roy went to the pastor to talk about it. This very mature and gentle man asked Roy if he had ever been disappointed by God's seeming lack of response to one of his prayers. Instantly, Roy remembered how he had prayed and prayed when he was a boy for God not to allow his grandfather to die. Back then, a pastor had told Roy that God had chosen to call his grandfather home because God wanted him to be with him. Roy wanted his grandfather to be with *him*. Roy's anger at God was really old. The pastor listened and was able to hear and accept Roy's pain and sadness about that early death. And as he talked, Roy felt his burden lift. A trigger was transformed.

When we own our own reactions to triggers, we stop blaming. This may allow others to stop being defensive and to start being understanding. We find that people are more likely to be supportive when they hear honest acceptance of another person's responsibility. Owning our own triggers is, in fact, a matter of owning our own story. We stop denying the past and we accept the emotions that we carry inside. Doing this leads us to the next important stage of transformation—finding meaning in the pain.

Finding Meaning in the Pain

Finding meaning in our pain means that we stop blaming the past or the present for all of our pain and we start understanding how we can learn and grow from all of our life experiences, including the painful ones. We find that it is very easy to get stuck in an endless cycle of reliving the past. In an attempt to understand the pain of the past, it is tempting to rehearse it. When anyone lives in the past world of hurts and wounds, he or she will often feel perpetually angry. They are long-term victims. These people might think, *If only I had come from a different family or different set of circumstances, then my life would be so much better.* Of course, that is a natural inclination for all of us. It is the "if only" syndrome. If only this or that had been better, I would be happier and more content.

We believe it is important to understand all of the pain from the past. It is vital to know how our memories affect us by causing us to have certain core beliefs, meanings, and perceptions. That pain can trigger us into all kinds of reactions. In this sense our pain is totally unique to us. The circumstances of pain are different for everyone.

But if pain is unique, it is also shared. One of our great spiritual teachers, Henri Nouwen, says that when we look at the uniqueness of our pain and wish those circumstances had been different, we miss the opportunity to realize that our pain is part of the universal experience of pain in the world.[1] Nouwen calls the universal experience of pain, "The Pain." Do you know anyone who hasn't experienced some problem or hardship at least at some time in their life? Would you not agree, then, that all of us to greater and lesser degrees have some kind of pain in our lives? That is the general human condition of suffering.

Jesus, who is the Son of God but was also a man, experienced the human condition of suffering. In fact, we Christians believe that he not only experienced it, he also took all of it to the cross and defeated the power of sin in all of our lives. Even before the cross, Jesus experienced the emotional abuse of Jewish leaders around him, the abandonment of his own disciples when he was in the Garden of Gethsemane, and the physical torture of Roman soldiers. Then Jesus knew the agonizing death on the cross and the feeling of being abandoned even by God. Jesus could have chosen another fate, but then he wouldn't have obeyed the will of his Father.

When we acknowledge that our pain, unique as it is, is the pain of all humanity and that Jesus knew everything about that pain, we can begin to understand what Jesus said in Matthew 11:29–30: "Take my yoke upon you and learn from me, for I am gentle and humble in heart, and you will find rest for your souls. For my yoke is easy and my burden is light."

On the surface it would seem rather impossible for any of us to take on Jesus' burden. It was the salvation of the world. The word *yoked*, however, is the key. When we are yoked we share a burden. For us, Jesus shares our burden. Whatever our pain, Jesus is familiar with it. We can share our pain and burdens with him, and he will help us to feel that it is lighter. We can also be yoked with someone we love and share our pain with him or her—and it will seem as if our burden is lighter.

Have you ever had the experience of sharing a problem or a painful feeling with another person, and when you did, the burden you carried became much lighter? When Mark counsels men, many times they will start out by saying, "I have never told this to anyone." It may be about some sin that occurred years and years ago. Mark can see the look of relief on a man's face when he surrenders the secret. When a man does that, his burden becomes lighter.

We know countless people who today look back on the painful experiences they've had and are even thankful for them. This may sound absurd, but they describe the meaning they make out of the pain. Without the pain they would not have grown and matured in their understanding of God, of life, and of relationships. James tells us this when he says, "Consider it pure joy ... whenever you face trials of many kinds, because you know that the testing of your faith develops perseverance" (James 1:2).

For example, Damian's critical father left him searching for father figures and a heavenly father. At first he thought that God was also critical and he could not go to church. With the help of his pastor, Damian made the association of pain he felt for his father for the pain he felt with God. Together, they talked about disconnecting that association. The pastor spoke a great deal of truth into Damian about how loving God really is. Gradually he came to see that God really was different. In large part, the gentleness and love of the pastor modeled a different kind of man. Today, Damian has transformed his pain into knowledge of a loving and gracious God.

Jeremiah's father physically beat him with a belt. For years Jeremiah thought that it was normal. When his son became the same age at which he was beaten, Jeremiah felt the temptation to use a belt on him. He discussed this with his father. His father apologized to him and said that those beatings were really about his own anger at being beaten as a child. By confessing and sharing, Jeremiah's dad bestowed a blessing on him. Today when his son misbehaves, Jeremiah knows how to be firm and yet tender and loving as well. In addition Jeremiah has a much deeper relationship with his father. He has transformed his pain into being a loving and wonderful son and father.

Sophie had many sexual relationships before marriage. The pain of her guilt was almost enough to cause her to call off the marriage. Courageously she shared her history with her fiancé. She also shared how triggered she got when she went to church and felt like a hypocrite. Her courage gave her fiancé the freedom to also confess many earlier sexual experiences. Today they have forgiven each other and themselves. In all aspects of their relationship they are much more intimate. In knowing that their mutual early sexual sin was not healthy spiritually and emotionally, Sophie and her husband have been able to find a much deeper love. Consequently, together they have transformed their sexual relationship into one that is a real expression of being "one flesh."

These are short and simple stories of the hundreds that we know. They are not simple, however, in that the pain of the experiences led all of these people to stronger faith in God and dependence on him and others. The time in which it took them to come to that place involved extensive examining of their lives, sharing their stories, and grieving their losses.

Healthy, Proactive Behaviors

When the victim of abuse or the person racked with guilt from his own bad decisions finds meaning in his experience, he becomes a survivor. Survivors don't blame others for their pain, and they stop feeling sorry for their situations. Instead, they become proactive, setting boundaries and asking for what they need.

Survivors learn how to create healthy boundaries. If a trigger is about something that is abusive, they can feel safer by knowing that they have choices about that situation. For example, Kirsten was very triggered by her brother's verbal abuse. He would call her names and blame her for things she didn't do. As the younger sister, she often didn't feel like she had any choice but to take it. But today, as an adult, she knows she does have choices to create safe boundaries. While her brother may still slip into verbal abuse, she can identify her trigger of fear and anger and decide to leave his presence. She knows today that she does not have to be a victim.

Survivors also learn to ask for what they need. After they have been triggered and they have identified their hurt, they will take another step to emotional health by figuring out what they need. You will notice that whenever survivors clearly ask for what they need, they state one of the seven desires. Kirsten identified her trigger of hurt when people spoke disrespectfully to her or blamed her. She needed to feel safe. She knew she had choices to leave or ignore those comments. And then she learned how to be proactive and state her needs in a conversation: "In order to stay here and talk with you and feel safe, I need you to stop blaming me." Kirsten also found other people in her life that listened to her and were affirming. They cared for her without judgment.

Today, Kirsten has found meaning in the pain of her childhood experiences with her brother. God is using that experience to grow her up emotionally and spiritually. She has examined her current trigger to know that her anger about verbal abuse and blaming statements is very old in her life. She also knows that she is not the helpless little girl that she was when those behaviors first occurred, and that now she has choices to respond differently to abusive situations. While she also believed that *she* was the problem when she was small and she was a bad person, she knows the truth about herself today: she is a good woman, deserving of love and safety. She also knows how to create safety for herself by looking at her choices when in abusive situations. She is much more resourceful. And she is able to speak up for herself and ask for what she needs or wants rather than hiding or running away—her old way of coping with verbal abuse. Kirsten is also depending on God to help her with the powerlessness of feeling afraid when her fear about an abusive situation occurs. Kirsten has grown by transforming her trigger.

Anointings

Triggers are like beacons of light that expose our pain. We cannot heal pain that we cannot identify and talk about. Debbie has actually renamed "trigger" for herself so that it doesn't symbolize something annoying that she wants to do away with. She uses the word "anointing" instead, meaning a blessing of sorts. When we are "anointed" by a stimulus that opens up a wounded place, we can then begin to understand it, heal from it, and make changes. We experience empowerment and growth when we don't let a trigger control our behavior.

In Debbie's book *Shattered Vows* she talks about women dealing with husbands who have sexually betrayed them. For these women, getting triggered by their feelings of harm happens all the time, particularly in the first year after they discover the betrayal. These women, hopefully, will go through the process we are describing here. Debbie has worked with hundreds of women, and has come to understand that when triggers become transformations, they are "anointings."

When we seek to share this "anointing" process with a friend, family member, or spouse, we become safe people to be with. Safe people can be companions: companions in the journey and companions in the pain. Companions experience a level of intimacy that is a precious gift.

Forgiving Those Who Hurt Us

The ultimate act of healing from the pain of the past is to forgive those who have hurt us. People of faith should know a lot about forgiveness. Most of us know, however, that it is much easier to want forgiveness and even ask for it than it is to give it to others. In one of the many challenging parables in the Gospels, Jesus tells of a servant who asks his master for forgiveness only to turn around and not forgive someone who owed him a debt. About this Jesus says:

> "Then the master called the servant in. 'You wicked servant,' he said, 'I canceled all that debt of yours because you begged me to. Shouldn't you have had mercy on your fellow servant just as I had on you?' In anger his master turned him over to the jailers to be tortured, until he should pay back all he owed.
>
> "This is how my heavenly Father will treat each of you

unless you forgive your brother from your heart." (Matthew 18:32–35)

Those of us who follow Christ have a clear set of instructions that we need to forgive. Even Jesus, after being tortured and crucified, forgave his torturers and those who had abandoned him as he hung on the cross when he said, "Father, forgive them, for they do not know what they are doing" (Luke 23:34).

The process of understanding the desires we have and the ways we have coped when they have not been met helps us to grow in our understanding of forgiveness. If we accept that we have yearned for things that we have not been able to have—being understood, affirmed, blessed, kept safe, touched, chosen, and included—and that we have coped with that sadness, hurt, or anger in hurtful ways in relationship, then we are ready to see how others may have also been doing the same thing. We can see others' behaviors, the stories of their lives, with different eyes. We can make a decision about the intent of their heart. We could decide that his or her behavior was not malicious, but self-protective. Their behaviors, as hurtful as they were, may have been the best that they were able to do. Just as we seek forgiveness and grace for our hurtful behaviors, we can now learn to serve others with the same. We can let go of our judgments.

Many of us were wounded by our parents and have since become parents ourselves. We are parents and are very proud of all of our children. We know that we have made lots of mistakes and that some of those mistakes have wounded them. Early along the way of our journey as parents, we found that it was good to admit our mistakes to our kids when we made them. Some people told us that the kids would use those apologies against us. That was never the case. We hope that they too will be people who know how to admit their mistakes when they make them.

Along the way we have also made mistakes and hurt friends, relatives, and the people we have served in ministry and counseling. What is clear to us is that if we expect to be forgiven by our children and these others, we need to forgive those who hurt us.

It is really important to know that we haven't always felt like forgiving. Hurt, anger, and resentment die hard. Our wounded selves have often sought to perpetuate our feelings as we "deserve to have them." But holding on to our feelings of anger and resentment only hurts us, not the other people. One of Mark's favorite authors, Frederick Buechner, puts it this way: "Of the Seven Deadly Sins, anger is possibly the most fun. To lick your wounds, to smack your lips over grievances long past, to roll over your tongue the prospect of bitter confrontations still to come, to savor to the last toothsome morsel both the pain you are given and the pain you are giving back in many ways is a feast fit for a king. The chief drawback is that what you are wolfing down is yourself. The skeleton at the feast is you!"[2]

We also used to think that the other person should come to us and ask for forgiveness. He or she should take responsibility for the wrong done and demonstrate understanding of the harm created. We spent lots of time longing for that kind of recognition. We learned, however, that the act of forgiving was something that we needed to do for ourselves. In some cases the people we needed to forgive no longer live near us. Some are even dead. It is interesting how we can hold on to anger and resentment against even those who have died.

As you work on how to forgive others who have harmed you, we encourage you to think about what it feels like to be forgiven yourself. So often we think that forgiveness can be done quickly and without much preparation. But we find that meaningful and lasting forgiveness takes time. If you have not first experienced what it is like to be forgiven and to receive God's wonderful grace, it is going to be very difficult to genuinely give that to someone else.

And if receiving grace is so important to the process, then you will have to know what you are receiving grace for—in other words, what have been *your* hurtful or sinful behaviors? Coming to terms with what your true nature has been and how you may have hurt others in major or minor ways can take some time. When you are hurting, it is hard to examine yourself to know how you have hurt someone else. So take your time to think about all of these things. When you are ready to *decide* to let go of your bitterness and judgment and to forgive another, you truly will feel free.

The real message of this chapter is that triggers are not an experience to avoid. They are, instead, opportunities to grow and mature spiritually and emotionally. When we own our own triggers, we accept responsibility for our reactions. We stop blaming others. We find meaning in them. We forgive those who caused us to have them. We become anointed by them.

We have explained the levels of the Iceberg Model, how we get triggered, and what we can do about it. In the next chapter, you will learn how to use the Iceberg Model to really understand the seven desires of your heart.

Points to Ponder

Please note: because of the serious nature of these questions, working through them could take weeks, months, or years.

⟩ Identify someone with whom you can safely share your burdens—a spouse, friend, relative, or counselor. Talk with them about your triggers. How do you feel after sharing your hurt?

⟩ Reflect on your painful life experiences. How can you find meaning in them and transform them into anointings?

⟩ Look back at the charts in chapter 3 (pages 59 and 62). If you haven't done so already, identify those who hurt you in the past, either through abandonment or invasion. Then spend time praying for forgiveness for each person named.

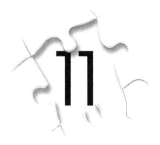

USING THE
ICEBERG MODEL

Just as only a portion of who we are is seen or known,
so an iceberg has much of its beauty
and character hidden beneath the water's surface.

Mark and Debra Laaser

The Iceberg Model can help you reframe many of your unrealistic expectations; reinterpret your distorted perceptions, meanings, and beliefs; allow you to have honest and congruent feelings; and avoid unhealthy coping behaviors. In so doing, the possibility of satisfying the desires of your heart greatly improve. You will be more available for intimacy in your important relationships. You will experience a new level of contentment and fulfillment. You will grow in your relationship with God. These are bold claims, we know, but we have seen it work in our own lives, and we see it work in the lives of people we work with every day.

Let's look at how the Iceberg Model could be applied to an everyday situation between a married couple, Olga and Nick. Bear with us as we go into detail a bit; our aim is to teach you how to use the model, so you can begin applying it to your own situations.

Olga and Nick

Early in the week, Olga asked her husband, Nick, to spend the day with her on Saturday. She planned to drive to the country, choose a quaint place to eat, and enjoy the turning of the fall leaves. Nick had agreed to go on the excursion.

Saturday morning arrived and Olga was eager to get going by 9 a.m. She had made coffee for the trip and had packed a few things to enjoy during the day. Nick, however, was still sleeping at 10. In fact, he didn't arise until 11 a.m., and then told Olga that he had to take care of a few emails. An hour later he had flipped on the TV to catch the beginning of a football game. Olga asked sarcastically if he thought he could be ready to go sometime before it got dark. He replied that he needed to get dressed and have a cup of coffee and then he'd be ready.

By now, Olga was fuming mad on the inside, so she grabbed a cup of coffee and said she was leaving by herself. Nick asked her if she couldn't wait just five more minutes while he got dressed. She said, "No, I've waited long enough! I'm leaving." Their day together was ruined, and they both ended up coping individually: she by isolating and withdrawing, he by watching TV all afternoon.

We helped Olga use the Iceberg Model to understand what she was really thinking and feeling. We walked her through the situation, talking about it with the help of Iceberg Model questions. Here is the result of her process:

> The *behaviors* she saw: Nick choosing sleep, emailing, and TV instead of her.
>
> When she saw these behaviors, her *feelings* were: anger, sadness, frustration, and loneliness.
>
> When she felt these feelings, she *coped* by: withdrawing and not talking about her feelings and being sarcastic; leaving/isolating/sarcasm.

The *distorted meaning* she made of Nick's behaviors was: he doesn't value me; he doesn't want to be with me.

The *distorted beliefs* she made about herself were: I am not important; I am not choosable.

Her *past story* that created painful memories for today: Olga's dad was a traveling salesman who was rarely home. When he was there, he was so distracted with helping Olga's mom that he never had time to play with her. He would start things with her and then disappear, only to be working on a home repair or something else. She never felt important enough to have his time.

Her *expectations (realistic or unrealistic)* were: if she invited Nick to go somewhere with her and he agreed, then he would be enthusiastic and timely.

Her *desire* was: to be chosen and to be included in Nick's life.

The *truth* about Olga: she was choosable and important. Other people's choices did not discount her value.

The *truth* about Nick's behaviors could be any number of possibilities, and she would need to check it out with him, but it could include: he was really tired from an exhausting week at work; while he wanted to go with Olga, he had forgotten that his favorite football team was playing that afternoon; he didn't realize how far Olga had planned to go and he was just expecting a couple of hours of time for their outing; he loved being with Olga but was afraid of her reaction if he said no because he didn't really want to go.

When Olga was able to reframe her truths and the *possibilities* of truths for Nick, she was able to consider alternative choices that day. She no longer was angry, sad, or lonely and therefore did not go into her coping behaviors. She was able to think and act from her congruent place of knowing she was valued and choosable. Here were her ideas for how she could have done this differently:

I could have shared with Nick my story of being neglected by my dad so that he would understand my feelings when plans don't work out.

I could have talked to Nick the night before about when we would leave and how long we would be gone to see if that was all right with him.

If he didn't get up, I could have gently asked him if he was still willing to go.

If he was tired, I could have offered to drive and to bring along coffee for him.

Seeing that he was obviously tired, I could have suggested we go another time or invite a girlfriend to go along instead.

When she did have a conversation with Nick about that day and what she might have done differently, he apologized for what had happened and assured her that it had nothing to do with not wanting to be with her. He said he was really distracted after a meeting with his boss the day before and could not sleep that night. He had no intentions of neglecting her desire to be together.

By talking about her story and her feelings and looking at possible solutions, Olga was actually choosing herself. And paradoxically, by choosing herself, she was able to stay present and not leave or withdraw so that Nick could hear her desire and make a decision to serve her (and thus also choose her).

Let's look at a few more examples to show how the Iceberg Model can be applied. By reading through these examples, you'll get a better idea of how to apply the model to your own situation.

Carol

Carol is sixty-five. Her husband died of a heart attack several years ago. Her children and grandchildren have gathered around her regularly, and she attends a wonderful church. When her husband first died, her family doctor prescribed a mild sedative for her. It did calm her down and she started liking the feelings it gave. Now she can't seem to stop taking them and gradually has seemed to need more and more.

Carol's outward *behavior* is that of chemical dependency. She has become addicted to her medication.

Carol is *coping* with her *feelings* of sadness, loneliness, and anxiety. These are totally normal to the grieving process. Often, however, she feels rather angry with herself, *a feeling about a feeling*, believing that she should be over it by now.

Carol's *core beliefs* are that strong people carry on and don't let even the most painful of losses interrupt their lives. She perceives that she is weak if she just can't function.

Carol *expects* herself to appear strong to others. This expectation won't allow her to get help from anyone else.

The *truth* is that Carol desires to be safe in the world and is lost without her husband. He is the one who chose her and included her. He was the main source of touch for her for all those years. He was a good listener, affirming, and a blessing in her life. Losing the most important person in her life leaves her wondering how to replace this source of getting her desires met.

As Carol has learned to use the Iceberg Model, she has started to talk openly to trusted people about her ongoing feelings of sadness, loneliness, anger, and anxiety, and her grieving process has continued in a healthy way. Several of her friends shared stories with Carol of how they had grieved the loss of a loved one. Her pastor has encouraged her that her feelings are not a sign of a lack of faith or that she is weak. Gradually, her doctor helped her cut down on her medication, and she is now completely free of it. Carol is getting out more and being more social. By getting honest and understanding the deep desires of her heart and talking about them, Carol is learning how to get them met in new ways.

For the most part it was culture that taught Carol she needed to be strong. Culture gave her a set of core beliefs—but she is now starting to revise those beliefs. Friends and family members are modeling the skill of talking about feelings. Gradually Carol is learning that by being honest about her feelings, she is really being much stronger than by keeping them to herself.

Curtis and Justine

Curtis hates his job. His boss is a real dictator. The stress of his job is wearing him down. When he comes home at night, he mostly wants to watch TV. Recently he bought the newest game system so that he can play several games he really enjoys. He didn't tell his wife, Justine, about it. He rationalizes that it is something that he and his three boys can do together.

Justine thinks that all computer games are evil. She is furious with Curtis for buying the game, particularly without asking her. She quotes Scripture to him and tells him that God is speaking to her that her house is possessed by something—the game system—that shouldn't be there. Justine can't stand being around Curtis right now, so she leaves the house for long periods. Sometimes she spends time with friends, during which time she complains about her husband.

When Curtis and Justine started using the Iceberg Model, they realized these things about themselves:

Curtis is *coping* with the stress of work by watching TV and by playing games. Justine is *coping* by blaming him and by leaving the house. She is using her faith in a rather self-righteous, super-reasonable way. She is also coping by sharing with her friends in ways that cause Curtis to feel betrayed.

Curtis is *feeling* a great deal of anxiety at work. He also has begun to feel anxious that he is always so anxious. When Justine reacts to his coping he feels shameful as well as angry. Justine is *feeling* very angry. She is also feeling angry that she has to be so angry! In many ways Justine feels like a victim or a martyr as she is the one who gets to deal with all three kids while Curtis spends so much time watching TV.

Curtis now knows that one of *his core beliefs* is that he can never get anything right. He experienced that from his dad and currently from his boss. He *perceives* that Justine doesn't think he is a man capable of making his own decisions. He also thinks her spirituality is self-righteous. Justine also *perceives* that Curtis doesn't care, as he makes all the financial decisions by himself. Justine also remembers that as the youngest child in her family, she always felt like the baby of the family whose opinion was never taken seriously and who was never included in many family conversations. *Her core beliefs* about herself are that she is not smart or spiritual enough to be listened to.

Curtis *expects* Justine to understand and to not be so angry. He feels entitled to a little relaxation. Justine *expects* him to help around the house and to spend more time in healthy ways with the family. She also expects Curtis to be the Christian leader of the home, and wishes that he would not bring such evil into the home—the new game system.

Curtis *desires* to be affirmed for his hard work. He wants Justine to hear and understand how difficult his boss is and how stressful his day really is. One of the ways he wants to be heard is that he is trustworthy to make decisions about game systems and that he is trying to bond with his boys. Justine *desires* to be included in decisions like this. She would also like to be affirmed for her spiritual intuition. She would feel chosen if Curtis trusted her opinion.

With these awarenesses, Curtis and Justine have begun to have healthy conversations. Their understanding of each other has grown. They have agreed to check in with each other daily, and have even started praying together for the kids and for the safety of their home. Curtis has agreed to limit his use of the game system to several hours per week, and Justine has decided to trust him that he won't play games that are harmful to him or to the kids. The *truth* is that they really love each other. They have started to see past their triggers, their old beliefs, and the ways they cope. They will still have to practice having safe conversations about all of these things, but they now have hope.

Isabella

Isabella is a single mother who is raising two sons, Harry, fourteen, and William, ten. Recently, she has discovered that Harry has been having problems in school. Harry's teacher has requested a school conference. The teacher asks Isabella if she has seen the notes about this that she has been sending home with Harry for the last month. Isabella has not seen them and so she goes into his room to look for them. She finds the notes—and she also finds an empty package of cigarettes.

Isabella is devastated. Before she confronts Harry, she uses the Iceberg Model to evaluate how she is doing and to decide how to work with her son about this problem.

The *problem* is obvious: Harry's school performance and his apparent smoking.

Isabella recognizes that she *feels* sad about this. She also knows that she is anxious, worried about Harry in school, and worried for his health. Her feelings of anxiety and worry lead her to feel angry. She is angry at herself for not noticing this earlier, angry at Harry for his deception, and angry at her former husband for not being involved in Harry's life. She knows that Harry must be feeling frightened about all of this because he has hidden the notes and tried to conceal his smoking.

The *meaning* that Isabella makes of all of this is that she is a "bad" mother." "Good" mothers don't have children who do poorly in school and who smoke. Her *perception* is also that Harry is being rebellious and that he must be depressed. Isabella wants to deal with this situation without creating more shame for Harry than she thinks he already has.

Her *expectations* have been that both of her boys be completely honest with her. She also expects her former husband to get involved. She wonders what Harry's expectations are and if he really thought she wouldn't find out about this.

Isabella *desires* to be safe—safe that her son won't continue to smoke. She also desires to be affirmed over the years as a mother. Harry also will want to feel safe—safe that his mother won't be too angry at him. He also desires to be more included in his father's life.

When they do meet with the schoolteacher, Isabella finds out that Harry has been having trouble with several of the other boys at school. These boys, says the teacher, are teasing him and challenging him to be a "real man" and smoke. The teacher feels that Harry is just trying to avoid conflict by going along with the smoking, and that the stress of the situation has affected his school performance.

Later, when Isabella talks with Harry, she assures him that she loves him and that she is so sorry for the teasing he has been enduring. She tells him that she is proud of him for who he is. Isabella is *blessing* her son as she is loving him despite what he has done. This does allow Harry to feel *safe* even though there will be consequences. She includes him in the decision about how they are going to deal with this problem. She tells him that there will be a punishment, and together they talk about what that is going to be. Harry won't be allowed to play any of his video games for a month so that he can concentrate on his schoolwork.

Isabella asks Harry if he would like to talk with his father about these issues, and she finds out that he is really sad about how little time his father spends with him. Without criticizing his father, Isabella shares with him how sad she is too. Together they decide that they will call him and ask him to come over to talk about this. They are *including* the father in the situation.

In these stories we have tried to give you some fairly common examples. We are aware that some of you may relate to these situations and some of you may not. We have only used these stories to illustrate the principles of using the Iceberg Model. Do you begin to see how you can take any problem and work your way down to the deep desires in your heart and the real truth about yourselves? We hope that these stories inspire you to look at some of the problem behaviors in your life and in your relationships. Ultimately, we hope that by understanding the deepest desires in your heart, you will focus on those and not on the problems on the surface that are really only symptoms of the pain that is caused when your desires are not being met.

In the next two examples, we are going to list the Iceberg questions in a very simple format. In these two stories, we will answer the questions for you. You can use this format as a way of examining your own situations.

Desiree

The holidays have always been a challenge for Desiree. When she was a child, Christmas traditions were very elaborate and included numerous family members. As a working mom with two little children, she was pressed for time and money to do everything she wanted to do to make the holiday special. She was also embarrassed by her house and her lack of time to take care of it the way she wanted. As holidays approached, she got very overwhelmed by her to-do list, and eventually took out her anger and frustration on her family. Initially, she was not able to talk about what was going on inside, but with the help of the Iceberg questions, she became aware of many of her thoughts and feelings. She was then able to talk to her family about these deeper issues and to create possibilities for solutions.

What is the *problem/behavior*? There is not enough time or money to prepare for the holidays.

What are your *feelings* when this problem/behavior occurs? I feel angry that no one is helping; I feel hopeless that I can't accomplish what I want to do.

How have you *coped* with these feelings? I yell at my kids; I am critical of my husband; I do not even like who I have become.

What is your *perception and meaning* of the problem/behavior? My kids and husband are lazy; they don't care about making the holidays special.

What is the *distorted core belief* that you create about yourself? If they cared about me and loved me, they would help.

What are your *expectations*? Of herself: I should be able to get things done, even though I work and raise children. Of her family: They should see what needs to get done and just pitch in.

What are the *desires* you long for? I want to be affirmed for what I do; I want to be praised for being a good mom and wife; I want to be safe (meaning freed from anxiety, and freed from having to take care of everything myself).

What is the *truth* about you and the truth about the problem? About herself: I do a wonderful job of making holidays special for my family and I work very hard. About the problem: My family is not always as cooperative as I would like, but they do contribute to helping with preparations; my expectations are too unrealistic given the careers both of us have and the ages of our children.

What are some *possibilities for change*? I could lower my expectations for an immaculate house and homemade meals. I could hire someone to help with the work that needs to be done. I could be more specific about when and where family members can help. I could take a few vacation days from work so as to have more time to prepare.

By walking herself through the Iceberg Model and talking to her family, Desiree gained some fresh insights and had some good ideas about preparing for the holidays. The kids agreed to help more if they could have a list of exact things their mom needed them to do. With the input of her family, Desiree was able to let go of needing totally cleaned-up rooms that would not be seen by company coming to visit. Desiree's husband agreed to hire sitters for several evenings so the two of them could do some of the shopping—and relaxing. All in all, Desiree enjoyed her holiday season more than ever before. She was proud that she did not once revert to angry outbursts or criticism of those she loved.

Sarah and Deb

The Iceberg Model can be used between adults and children. We'll illustrate by telling you a story that involves Deb and our daughter Sarah, who was then five and in her first semester of kindergarten.

The bus came to pick up Sarah each morning to take her to school. Her younger brother, Jon, was just two and stayed home with Deb. One morning, Sarah got dressed for school as usual, but just before the bus arrived, she started crying uncontrollably and refused to go to school. The Iceberg Model helped Deb talk to Sarah about what was really going on.

What is the *problem*? Sarah didn't want to go to school.

What are you *feeling*? Sarah's reply: "I am angry and sad that I have to go to school and Jon gets to stay home."

How was she *coping*? Sarah was close to having a tantrum, a meltdown—she was crying uncontrollably.

What do you think about not getting to stay home? Sarah's *perception*: "You are going to have fun with Jon and I won't get to join you."

What do you *believe* about that? "I never get to be with you [Mom] alone and have fun like Jon does."

Her *desire* (from Deb's perspective): Sarah wanted to be included and chosen.

After acknowledging Sarah's feelings, Deb asked, "What would help you feel better about that?" (possible solutions). Sarah proposed, "I want to skip school and do something with you [Mom] all by myself." Deb's alternative: "What would you think about having Dad take care of Jon on Saturday, and you and I will spend the day together doing something special?"

Final remarks/behaviors: "OK!" And off she went to catch the bus.

The problem is never the problem—there are always deeper parts of us that need to be explored. Now that you are beginning to understand how to use the Iceberg Model, we will turn our attention more fully to how you can serve yourself with it and also how you can serve the desires of others.

Points to Ponder

This is a much longer section than earlier Points to Ponder. We think that at this point in the book, you might be ready for a really challenging opportunity to learn how to use what you are learning.

What "above the line" problems do you deal with today? We encourage you to practice the Iceberg Model by yourself. Here are some basic ways to do that:

- ❥ Write down the problem or the behavior you see on paper in one sentence, or say it to yourself in one sentence.

- ❥ Ask yourself how you feel when this problem comes up. If you need to consult a list of feelings, like the one we have included on page 93, do so. You can write the feelings down if you want to.

- ❥ Make a list, in your mind or on paper, of how you think you cope. Consult the possibilities that we listed earlier. Try to be as specific as you can.

- ❥ When this problem comes up, what perceptions do you have and/or what meanings do you make about it?

- ❥ How does this problem make you feel about yourself? Describe what (distorted) core belief you have created. Think back to similar problems in the past, even as far back as your original family, and think of stories of how this problem was handled by your parents or other authority figures around you. Do you have any religious beliefs about this problem?

▶ What expectations do you have of yourself, of others, or from God concerning this problem?

▶ Which of the seven desires do you find this problem challenges?

▶ What is the truth about the behavior/problem and about you?

▶ What are possibilities for solving this problem/behavior?

If you are having a problem with someone else, you can also practice the Iceberg Model with a friend, relative, or spouse. Here are some ideas about how to do that:

▶ Ask the other person if he or she would be willing to sit down with you and have a healthy and safe conversation.

▶ State the problem as you see it in one or two sentences. Ask the other person if that is an accurate description of the problem.

▶ Take turns. Each one of you should go down through the levels of the model. If the other person doesn't know the model, give him or her a copy of it. Tell them that it will be easier to explain if he or she is willing to listen as you go through the stages.

➤ When you have talked about your feelings, your coping methods, your beliefs and perceptions, your expectations, and your desires, ask the other person to do the same.

➤ Be mindful of not interrupting. After you have talked about each level, ask the other person to repeat back what they heard. If they don't get it quite right, repeat what you said. Then, as they talk about each level, repeat back to them what you heard and make sure you got it right.

➤ Point out after you finish how similar both of you are in what you have described.

➤ Ask the other person how they feel about the problem at this point. Did the model help both of you glean new insights? Did the model help you distinguish the real problem from the observable, seeming problem?

➤ Be patient with yourself. Using the Iceberg Model takes a lot of practice. If you are practicing with yourself or someone else, be gentle with yourself and with the other person. If you get off track and emotions are getting heated, take a time out. Come back to it later and try again. If you are having too much difficulty, ask someone to listen to you or to the two of you. This usually serves to keep conversations relatively safe.

FULFILLING YOUR
OWN DESIRES

*[The Lord] satisfies your desires with good things
so that your youth is renewed like the eagle's.*
PSALM 103:5

Sierra was raised by a very critical mother and a busy and absent father. She was not affirmed or blessed as she was growing up. Today, Sierra works for a large company, and her immediate boss is a woman. Sierra longs to please her, but never feels like she does. Sierra is part of a team that includes a number of men, none of whom seem to take any of her contributions seriously. They are currently working on a project on which Sierra would very much like to do well in order to please her boss. She really needs her colleagues to help, but they are not driven like she is. She never feels that she is acknowledged for all the extra work she puts in on their project. And she never feels like her boss appreciates all she does for her either, or that she even likes her as a person. Sierra is constantly frustrated at work and is very anxious. She is wondering if she should look for a new job.

Throughout this book you have undoubtedly reflected on whether or not you received the seven desires when you were growing up. How are you doing? Did you receive them when you were little? Are you receiving them today? If you did not receive the seven desires as a young person, you will be yearning for them from everyone around you—especially from your spouse if you are married.

In Sierra's case, she longed for affirmation and blessing from everyone she worked with. In this chapter, we would like to teach you how to fulfill the desires of your own heart. Doing so may also help you with any unrealistic expectations you put on others, the consequence of not having your own desires met when you were little.

Have you noticed how you long to have the seven desires met by someone else? Have you taken account of how you cope when someone else doesn't meet your desires? Remember that you can cope individually and in relationship. Your individual coping is a false substitute and is not really satisfying, and your relational coping may drive others away from you.

Your coping may even sabotage your efforts to get your desires met. For example, Devyn desperately needed his wife to affirm him. He was always complaining that she didn't love or respect him. His wife got very tired of his complaints and withdrew more and more. So rather than affirming him for the good things that she noticed, she was now focused on figuring out how to cope with his constant anger. Devyn was actually sabotaging his ability to have his wife notice and affirm him.

You may notice that you have longed specifically for several of the seven desires. For instance, you may say, "I just really need affirmations." Or, "I wish I could find someone to trust (so I could feel safe)." Or, "I just want my husband to buy me nice things (and choose me)." You will yearn especially for those desires that you missed receiving while you were young. And before you look to other people to meet those desires, you need to bring your desires before God.

Here are some of our thoughts about how you can get your unmet desires fulfilled through your relationship with God.

Surrender Your Unmet Needs to God

It is easy to be angry about unmet needs and to blame others, especially parents, for that. We previously wrote about forgiving those who hurt you or let you down. We also talked about finding meaning in your pain. When you do these things, you are actually surrendering those needs to God. Doing so is a recognition that these needs may never get met, and that is up to God. For one thing, none of us can go back to being a child. Even if those who hurt us long ago change and start giving us the desires of our heart today, that still can't make up for what we lost earlier.

Surrendering to God involves recognizing that your attempts at false solutions really don't work. It also involves recognizing that you can't manipulate others into giving them to you. It is a letting go. It is a relief. And it is sad. Surrendering your unmet desires, particularly those from childhood, involves grieving. As you grieve, you will process the feelings you go through when you really realize that you have lost something — feelings such as anger, sadness, and fear. Grieving takes time.

To process grief, you need to talk about the loss to those who can relate and listen. When you talk about your loss, you may be surprised to find that many others have the same kind of feelings. They also know the anger, anxiety, and sadness of letting go. The strange paradox of this process is that you may find new fellowship in which you will find some of your desires met. Others will *hear* you, and if they have been through similar loss, will *understand*. They will *affirm* you for talking openly. They will accept you where you are and for whom you are — a real *blessing*. By talking to others and by them listening, you are mutually *including* each other in the process of grief.

Allow God to Serve You
in Ways That Only He Can

The Bible is full of God's promises to us. For example, the Psalmist frequently affirms that God hears us: "In the morning, O LORD, you hear my voice; in the morning I lay my requests before you and wait in expectation" (Psalm 5:3). Now there is a realistic expectation! Moses is instructed to tell the people, "The LORD bless you and keep you; the LORD make his face shine upon you and be gracious to you; the LORD turn his face toward you and give you peace" (Numbers 6:24 – 26). Not only are we promised that God blesses us, but he also keeps us safe. Can you imagine the face of God smiling on you? Is that not something you long for?

We know that in the midst of pain, it is hard to remember these truths about God. That is why we will often need to be around others who will remind us of the truth. It is also important to know that God works through other people. We can remember countless times when just the right person or people showed up for us to hear us or give us a kind word. Even as we write, we know that God blesses our work through the prayers of many people who support us.

Sometimes, by simply seeking to follow God and by meditating on who he really is, we are challenged to serve him and others. This may work to diminish our desires. God often reminds us of what is really important. We may desire to have that new material object, like a new car or a better house, but God points us in the direction of others and tells us that material objects don't satisfy.

We especially like those times when God is an "ever-present help in trouble" (Psalm 46:1). Do you know those moments when

God is very real? He does seem to listen and directly comfort just by the sense of his presence. Often we long for the loud voice of God to be very clear to us, but look at how God spoke to Elijah in 1 Kings 19:12. After the earthquake, fire, and storm, God spoke to him in a "gentle whisper."

We encourage you to build trust that God will provide for your desires in a variety of ways at a variety of times ... *not always in the way or time you were expecting.* When you fully trust God to provide, you can then accept what others will give you ... and it can be enough. Paradoxically, when your need to have your desires met by people around you diminishes, those that can serve you are more likely to do that! And you live with the assurance (and truths) that you will be okay, and that you are okay, despite how the desires come to you.

Practice Fulfilling Your Own Desires

Do you find that when you relate to others, for example your own children (if you have them), you are a good listener and that you understand? Do you know that you are affirming, and with those you love you do it unconditionally? Are you supportive and protective? Do you like to touch others in non-sexual ways? Are you good at helping to choose others and help them feel included?

Most of you can probably answer yes to at least one of those questions. Would it not be true then that you have the ability to fulfill desires? Even if you think you are not good at any of those things, do you recognize what it might be like to be able to fulfill the desires of others? Can you at least imagine what it would be like? The truth is that you probably have the ability and skills to fulfill yourself.

Listen to Yourself

Ask yourself a seemingly simple question: "Do I hear and understand myself?" When you are sad about something, do you let yourself be sad? When you are hurt by someone, do you speak up, voice your reality, and state your needs? One way you can practice listening to yourself is by identifying your feelings and needs and then stating them.

Have you ever said, "I knew better" or "I had a feeling about that"? Chances are you are not good at listening to yourself, particularly your intuitions. All of us have common sense wisdom. We often know answers to difficult problems; we just don't listen to ourselves. Our core beliefs, meanings, and perceptions of ourselves are that we just don't know. We just don't trust ourselves. The part of you that is wounded puts yourself down. The part of you that copes wants to search for the false solution. The voices inside you that speak to you from your shameful or anxious self are always defeating.

Sometime, try setting those voices aside and say, "If I did have wisdom, what would I tell myself?" Tell your wounded self and your coping self to be quiet for a moment. Imagine ignoring your shame and anxiety for at least a short time. Then listen to your true self, your wisdom. Trust that. At least try it.

You may find that God has a way of speaking to you when you quiet the negative parts of yourself. Someone once said, "Prayer is when we pray to God. Intuition is when God speaks to us." Are there not times when you "just had a feeling?" Later, you somehow knew it was from God. When you just know, you may find that your feeling is one of quiet confidence. Other people can embrace that "still, small voice of God" in you. This is not the super-reasonable coping stance where you appear or even have to sound like you know everything. It is not a self-righteous place. It is a self-assured, serene place. Do you ever long for more serenity in your life? Maybe this is how you find it.

Affirm Yourself

In the same way, do you affirm yourself when you are doing something well? Or do you mentally put yourself down? Your self-talk is a great way to observe whether you are actually affirming your own life. Too often we criticize or blame ourselves with our thoughts: *You are such an idiot! Why didn't you see that coming? If I weren't so slow at fixing things, we might not be in such a mess now. I can't ever seem to get it right—I'm just hopeless.* Can you hear the lack of affirmation that goes on inside your own brain?

How many negative messages from the past do you have inside your head? Dr. Daniel Amen, a great friend of ours, calls these voices "ANTs." That stands for Automatic Negative Thinking. How often do you tell yourself that you can't do it or you won't get it? You will often "parent" yourself the way you were parented. So if you heard many critical messages about yourself, you might be inclined to speak to yourself that way too. Some people don't experience being criticized themselves, but they hear a lot of criticism or judgment of others from their parents, pastors, or teachers. It is not unusual for those children to still take in a lot of messages about themselves as being inadequate.

Practice telling yourself the opposite message. Practice affirming yourself. There was an episode of a popular TV show in which one of the very negative characters decides to follow the exact opposite of whatever thought comes into his head first. During the show he winds up being successful at everything he does. Of course, if the writers of that show allowed him to stay that way, the show wouldn't have been so funny.

You might think about the fact that thinking negative thoughts has been a way of life for you. You don't know how to be different. That is why it is good to imagine and practice "as if" you knew how to do this.

Many of us just wait for others to notice and affirm in hopes that their reality will serve to change the beliefs we hold about ourselves. But you can find great contentment and change old distorted beliefs about who you are by consciously noticing and affirming yourself. You might also find that if you practice affirming others, you may start getting some affirmations back.

Remind Yourself of God's Unconditional Love and Blessing

How are you at blessing yourself? Do you really believe God's truth that you are worthy and precious and purpose-filled? If you can carry those truths with you wherever you go, you don't need to be so affected by what other people say to you or think about you. They do not need to stand on a pedestal above you, bumping you off your truth just because they have their own opinion. God's opinion is really the only one that matters. We would bless ourselves much more readily if we would remove earthlings from that pedestal and seek only the opinion and truth of God.

The Bible is totally clear that you are "fearfully and wonderfully made" (Psalm 139) and that God sent his only Son so that you who believe in him won't perish but have eternal life (John 3:16). Again, there may be old messages inside your head that prevent you from believing that God loves you. Thinking that you are not worthy may be a message that is so normal for you, that you actually resist the positive message because you wouldn't know what to do if you were blessed. If it is hard to look in the mirror and tell yourself that you are blessed, start by simply reading Psalm 139 and John 3:16 to yourself—aloud!

Remind Yourself That You Are in God's Hands — You Are Safe

You can continue to work on giving yourself safety by working on creating safe boundaries with those who harm you — either verbally, physically, sexually, or spiritually. You are an adult now, and although you may be triggered into feeling like you are very small and being hurt like you might have been as a child, it is now a new time. You do have the power today to take charge of your life and make a different choice to keep yourself safe.

You can also remember that God is in control. The Bible is full of reminders that we shouldn't be anxious. You say, "That is easier read than felt." We certainly know what you mean. The truth is that we are safe in God. Ask yourself this question: "If God was in charge, what would I do differently today?" In other words, what would you let go of trying to control? Try it.

Mark, who gets rather zealous about caring for our yard, experimented one year and didn't rake the leaves. The next spring, some of the leaves were still there, some of them were gone, and after mowing the grass a couple of times, we really couldn't tell the difference. The house and everyone in it were fine.

On a more practical note, you may have many concerns about your financial well-being. Do you have enough money? Are you informed enough about how to handle money? Is anyone else (like a spouse) not including you in decisions about family spending? You can make choices about what information you need to know and how you will earn money. And you can decide to let God help you accept what you have and depend upon him to provide opportunities if you need more money. You will still need to let go of control at times.

What can you let go of today? By practicing surrender, you will learn to let go of more significant fears in your life: for instance, your health, your career, or even the injustices of the world. Letting go is hard, but done intentionally, it can teach you to depend on God to keep you safe.

Safe Touch

You can also work on giving yourself healthy touch—even as a single person. You can learn to touch safe friends or family when you feel connected and you want to share that close feeling. A touch on the arm, a squeeze of the hand, or an arm around someone's waist can all be ways of sharing safe touch. The nice thing about hugs is that they are mutually reciprocal: you give one and automatically get one back. Virginia Satir once said that everyone needs four hugs a day to survive, eight to maintain health, and twelve to grow![1]

There are more simple ideas to receive safe physical touch. You may enjoy a warm bath or a pedicure or a shampoo at your local salon. Or treat yourself to a massage or a facial! Pets can provide us with incredible safe touch. No wonder so many of us enjoy coming home to the soft, furry welcome of our favorite animal—their snuggles and kisses are wonderful beyond words.

Choose Yourself

If choosing yourself sounds strange, maybe even selfish, ask yourself—right now—what meanings, perceptions, and core beliefs you have about this idea. In its simplest terms, choosing yourself means taking your own needs seriously. It is an encouragement especially for those who never do that because they are always thinking of the needs of others. They have learned to ignore their needs and even to believe they don't have them. They have given up on having needs. As you learn to choose yourself, you must first know what you need—knowing what you like or prefer.

So many people have no clue what they like. They have been pleasing others for so long that they rarely think about it. Start by asking yourself that question as you move through your day: Is there something I want to be doing that I am not doing? Or is there something I am doing that I want to stop doing? Start small and practice. Where do you like to eat? What movies or TV shows do you like to watch? Where do you like to go on vacation? What are your good ideas at work? How can you take time for yourself when everyone else seems to need you? Do you have enough information about your financial situation? Each time you make a conscious decision to know what you want and to follow through, you are choosing yourself.

You can also choose yourself by taking care of your body: make appointments for the doctor and the dentist, get your eyes examined, buy yourself clothes that fit and are attractive for you, get a haircut that is pleasing to you, allow yourself time to get enough sleep, choose healthy foods, and exercise.

You can choose yourself by listening to your passion and by creating a vision that supports it. You choose yourself when you are hurting and you decide to get help. You choose yourself when you say no if you really don't want to say yes. You choose yourself when you are not happy and you decide to do something about it. Every time you set aside the feeling of being a victim, you are choosing yourself.

Decide Where You Really Belong

Being included has a lot to do with whether you desire to be in community. You can include yourself by initiating. If you have only been a follower in your relationships, you set yourself up to be excluded. You are at the mercy of someone else leading you or including you. But you can change that by being proactive. You can decide what friendships you would like to develop; you can decide what organizations to join; you can decide to run for an office or volunteer for a job or train for an event. You can work diligently to include yourself!

Are there activities or groups that you participate in even though you don't like to? What anxiety prevents you from stopping? Where do you feel at home? We mean groups, churches, clubs, and organizations. For example, do you continue to go to a church just because you've gone there for a long time and yet you find it unfriendly? What family or friends have you not connected with lately? Make a call, write a letter or email, or invite someone over for coffee. One of the ways to include yourself is to invest in the relationships you already have.

It will take a lot of practice and patience to fulfill your own seven desires. Most of us simply are not used to creating our own contentment and value. Rather, we expect that others will be there to complete us and fill us up with the things that we need. Christians especially are often taught not to focus on ourselves. But we encourage you to learn to "love yourself as your neighbor" and to parent yourself with the seven desires, because you are worth loving and respecting no matter how others love and respect you.

The paradox is that as you begin to practice serving yourself with the seven desires, your need to have others give you what you long for will diminish. You truly begin to trust yourself and to trust God to give you what you need. And as your needs diminish, your unhealthy coping strategies will diminish as well. You will not need to comfort yourself with false substitutes or protect yourself from so much pain, because you will not be in so much pain! And as your unhealthy coping disappears, you will be a person who produces the fruit of the Spirit: love, joy, peace, patience, kindness, goodness, faithfulness, gentleness, and self-control (Galatians 5:22–23).

The wonderful conclusion to living like this is that people *want* to be around you—you are *approachable*. And they do come around to hear and understand you more, affirm you, bless you, show concern about your safety, touch you in respectful ways, choose you, and include you.

Points to Ponder

▶ As you look at your own life, which of the seven desires are you most lacking?

▶ In order to begin serving yourself with the seven desires, what internal messages will you need to confront? (For example: I am selfish if I do something for myself.)

▶ Which of the seven desires do you already fulfill for yourself?

▶ As you go through a day this week, stop to ask yourself about what you really like: for example, the breakfast food you're eating, your job, someone else's suggestion about where to go for lunch, what someone else wants to watch on TV.

▶ This is advanced level: Set up three chairs in one of the rooms of your house. Label one of them your wounded chair. Label the middle chair your coping chair. Finally, label the last chair your God chair or your wisdom chair. Now take a decision you face, however large or small, and ask yourself what decision you would make if you're sitting in the wounded chair. Now sit in the coping chair and ask yourself the same question. Last, sit in the God chair and quiet your thoughts. Ask yourself, "What is God telling me?" You might be surprised to see what different answers you come up with in each of the chairs. Finally, ask yourself, "What answer feels right?"

FULFILLING THE DESIRES
OF OTHERS

For even the Son of Man did not come to be served,
but to serve, and to give his life as a ransom for many.
MARK 10:45

This chapter focuses on how we can fulfill the desires of others — how we can be good listeners, be understanding, be affirming; how we can bless others, and create safety for others; how we can touch in non-sexual ways, express our desire for and our choice of others, and include others in our lives.

This is a tall order. In fact, people can fulfill others' desires only because God has shown us how. In Ephesians 5:1 – 2 Paul instructs us this way: "Be imitators of God, therefore, as dearly loved children and live a life of love, just as Christ loved us and gave himself up for us as a fragrant offering and sacrifice to God."

This passage reminds us of two things. First, we can't do any better than following God's example. We can never expect to be perfect, but Christ should be our example of what we strive to be like. Second, to be like Christ, we should be willing to sacrifice. To serve the desires of others may require sacrifice. We may not ever face dying for someone else, but we can become more selfless, compassionate, and empathetic.

Let's talk about this idea of sacrifice and selflessness for a minute. While Jesus did do many selfless acts and sacrificed his own life, he also acknowledged his own needs. There were times in his ministry when he did take time to care for himself. He did have friends. He played with children. He did take time away from the crowds. He did allow Mary to wash his feet with expensive ointment. He did ask his disciples to stay awake with him in the Garden of Gethsemane, even though they were not able to.

Think of those people whom you have admired over the years. Were they not people who gave of themselves unselfishly? Where would you be without someone who loved you enough to serve you? Even if there was no one really like this in your life, think of those we admire because of their sacrifice. We pay tribute to those who have served in the military because of their willingness to serve and to die for their country. During the days after 9/11 we came to wonder in awe at the sacrifice of those who died trying to serve and save others. Tom Brokaw called the generation that grew up during the Great Depression and fought World War II the "Greatest Generation." Millions of them served and died for their country without questioning it.

Serving and being sacrificial does not mean that you have to abandon your own desires. It *does* mean that you will have to first look to God, and only second to other people, to meet your desires. If you can trust that your own desires will be met, you can suspend your own needs at times so that you are available to serve others. When you can do that, then you will be ready to serve.

Recognize When You Are Depleted

It is hard to serve if you are stressed and tired. Perhaps life has been very difficult and you have been wounded in many ways. Perhaps your current life circumstances have stretched your resources. Perhaps you are living in a situation in which a person or the people around you continue to hurt you. If these things are true for you, you may find your personal energy severely depleted. You are so tired that you just don't have anything to give. If that is the case for you, you may want to get help from caring people such as family members who understand, friends who can listen to you and be understanding, a pastor, or a counselor. There is an old saying that for a well to overflow, it has to first be filled up. You may need to fill yourself up—or, better yet, let God fill you up—in order for your service to overflow to others.

If you find that serving others creates a feeling of being drained, it could be that there is something about the situation you are trying to serve that is not quite right. Feeling drained means that you are exhausted, overwhelmed, and depleted. Perhaps you need to attend to something in your own life first. It is not healthy to continue to give and give without taking care of yourself. This is called being a "martyr." Martyrs can often be angry about always giving and never receiving. Anger is not congruent with serving. Allow yourself some time to put good things into yourself before you try to serve others.

Feeling drained can also mean that you are doing something for other people that they could—and should—do for themselves. There are people who will allow you to serve them, even expect you to do so, when it might be better if they took care of their needs themselves. We use the word *enabling* to refer to this kind of serving. You may think that serving in this kind of situation leads to you being appreciated, but it is possible that you are being taken for granted. You find that you do and do, and it doesn't bring you the reward you desire. That is exhausting.

Being a servant means that you will need to separate out those situations where people really need your help from those in which they don't. You will also need to decide if you have enough healthy energy to be giving even when it is legitimately needed. Only when you feel renewed and strong are you ready to be a servant.

Serve from the Right Motivation

In addition to examining your energy before you serve, it is also important to examine your motivation because there can be times when it is unhealthy. If you serve others because it is the only way you feel valued, your motivation is not pure. Remember that one of the ways to cope is to placate, or to please others. Placating can look like serving, but it is done with the wrong motivation. It is selfish, not selfless. A Placater is serving out of fear of being alone or of being rejected. So she will give and give to others in hopes of pleasing them to stay. When a Placater attempts to serve others (or do for others), the recipient may not even want or need to be served. But the Placater serves anyway so as to feel better. A Placater will say yes even though she needs or wants to say no.

Virginia Satir came up with a wonderful image we like to use. Imagine that you have a medallion with the word *yes* on one side and *no* on the other. Keep the medallion with you to remind you that you can always say yes for the right reasons or no for the right reasons. There may be times when saying no might be just as much an act of service as saying yes. Saying no at times might keep you from getting too depleted and at the same time allow someone else the opportunity to do something they needed to do.

Maybe you are suffering from a "works righteousness" belief —that your serving will please God and assure your salvation. But the Bible tells us clearly that we do not need to earn our salvation. "For it is by grace you have been saved, through faith—and this not from yourselves, it is the gift of God—not by works, so that no one can boast" (Ephesians 2:8–9). So if you are driven by that kind of serving, your motivation is misguided. Those who worry about God's pleasure have a great deal of anxiety about the approval of others, including God.

Serving can become a competitive choice, in that your serving may be offered to outdo someone else—to look better than others. This is just another way of searching for affirmation by being the best servant. This too is the wrong motivation to serve.

If you are serving from the right motivation, you will be able to accept someone saying, "No thanks, I do not need your help." Or, "I really need to learn how to do this myself." You will not feel offended or unloved because someone has another need of their own that does not include your service.

If you have children, imagine how it would be if you did everything for them—their homework, their cleanup, their entertainment. You might think that you are serving their needs, but they would never learn how to do things on their own. Serving others when they do not need it or want it only handicaps them from acquiring skills of their own—to even have needs of their own! It is no wonder that so many adults don't even know what their own needs are. Either they were never allowed to have needs, or they were served so well that they never learned how to do anything for themselves. Remember to serve from the right heart.

Let Your Serving Be Unconditional

Perhaps your willingness to serve is conditional. In other words, you refuse to affirm someone if you are not being affirmed. You don't invite someone over to your house if you haven't been invited to theirs. You don't listen to someone else if you feel that all they do is talk. If you have unmet desires, you might withhold yourself from serving the desires of others. If you have been expecting others to meet all of your desires, you are probably angry because they haven't—and in that angry place, you are not ready to serve anyone anything. But true service is always unconditional. You need to be able to serve without expecting anything in return. This does not mean that you may not have some of your desires met while serving another. The difference is that you would be okay if they were not.

Hear a Person's Story

Sometimes we don't know how to serve because we don't know another person's needs or desires. We may simply not know, or the person we seek to serve may not know what their needs are. How could we, then, know? We find, instead, that it is often helpful to ask a person to tell us about their life. We often talk about a person's life as being their "story." A person's story can include their life history and their current life situation, their relationships, their work, their problems, and their feelings. Have you ever experienced how nice it feels to have someone sincerely ask about you and really seem interested in listening? In other words, they really want to *hear and understand* you. If you really know a person's story and understand them, you will be better able to serve them.

Andrew knew he needed to be able to tell his wife Martha that he chose her. He wasn't quite sure how to do that. He asked her to tell him what it was like for her when she was a girl, adolescent, and teenager. He heard stories from her about times when she went to the junior high dance and was not asked to dance, of not being asked to the prom, and of not getting into the sorority she wanted in college. Andrew decided, based on this information, to ask his wife on a date to go dancing. Although Andrew was embarrassed about his own dancing skills, he suspended his feelings about that to serve his wife. Andrew wanted to choose her.

Sometimes just asking another person to tell their stories is a great gift of service. Maybe the other person has never thought that anyone would be interested. He or she may have thought that no one would ever want to hear them. Just listening to the story may be an act of service.

Paradoxically, it could be an act of service to tell another person *your* story. Perhaps that person has always thought that she was the only one who ever had a certain thought or a certain experience. This could be particularly true of thoughts or experiences about which we feel ashamed. Sharing your story with others might help them to know that they are not alone. This could serve to reduce their guilt and shame. It might also give them the opportunity to tell you their story in return. All these things are a great gift of service.

Empathize with Others' Pain

If we are going to serve, we will need to have empathy for the person we seek to serve. That may mean that you do take time to hear their story. How can you empathize with another person's pain if you don't know the stories that created it? Often in the telling of stories we can identify with another person, because we have a similar story.

At a church-based accountability group, Roy got honest about his fear of judgment from the other men. Bill asked him if he knew why he didn't trust other men. Roy recounted that his dad was very harsh and critical. Bill responded that he understood—his dad had been the same way. Bill had empathy for Roy. By asking about his story and by identifying with it, he served Roy and helped him feel that maybe, just maybe, men could be safe.

The apostle Paul describes empathy in this way, "And our hope for you is firm, because we know that just as you share in our sufferings, so also you share in our comfort" (2 Corinthians 1:7).

Empathy is the act of identifying with another person's feelings. How can you empathize if you have never identified your own feelings? Some people expect to be empathetic before they have done the work of understanding their own story and their own feelings. This work of understanding yourself (and it *is* work!) isn't just a matter of rehearsing the past or feeling sorry for yourself. Nor is it selfish. You need to take time to understand your own desires, needs, feelings, and pain.

Jesus put it this way:

> One of the teachers of the law came and heard them debating. Noticing that Jesus had given them a good answer, he asked him, "Of all the commandments, which is the most important?"
>
> "The most important one," answered Jesus, "is this: 'Hear, O Israel, the Lord our God, the Lord is one. Love the Lord your God with all your heart and with all your soul and with all your mind and with all your strength.' The second is this: 'Love your neighbor as yourself.' There is no commandment greater than these." (Mark 12:28–31)

Many of us get the first part of that second commandment, "Love your neighbor." That is what this chapter is really about. We don't focus, however, on the second part, "as yourself." To be empathetic, we will need to take time for ourselves: to read, study, get counseling, journal, meditate, talk to trusted friends. As we love ourselves in these ways, we will become ready to love others. We won't be depleted or angry; we will be available.

Decide to Serve

Many people wait to serve others with the seven desires until they feel like doing it. We find that this can be a long wait. After all, you might never feel like serving others! So often the ability to serve depends on a conscious *decision* to serve. A decision will lead to action, and the action may in turn foster positive feelings about serving.

Peter's wife always wanted to go on a cruise, but Peter hated the thought of being confined on a boat. He was afraid of being seasick and resisted the idea for years. Finally, as their twenty-fifth anniversary approached, Peter decided to surprise his wife with a cruise. He wanted to affirm her need by choosing to fulfill her heart's desire. Peter dreaded the cruise, but he enjoyed the thought of pleasing his wife. Strangely, Peter found that he loved the cruise. As they left the ship, Peter said, "That was wonderful. I'm so sorry that I resisted it so long. Let's do it again next year."

Mary and her husband Tom had fought about the frequency of sex for years. He always seemed to want more. Mary got angry at the demands, and Tom got angry at the resistance. Then, around their twentieth anniversary, Tom decided that his love for Mary really didn't depend on sex and that he loved her for her spirit. Mary remembered that when she allowed herself to be sexual she did really enjoy it. She decided to say yes more often and perhaps even to initiate. As Tom affirmed his love, he became less demanding. As Mary decided to say yes, she enjoyed sex more. Today their frequency is never an issue. When they do have sex it has become a deeper emotional and spiritual time of connecting. They both made a decision to serve the other.

Raymond didn't like his boss. He thought she was too demanding and often critical. He found that he would procrastinate and allow himself to be careless. One day he decided that he was only hurting himself and the company, so he began to try harder. Gradually he found a deeper sense of pride in doing his job well. Strangely, his boss became less critical and demanding and even occasionally gave him a compliment.

We have been encouraging you throughout this book to identify your feelings, to express them, and to feel them. There are times, however, when we urge you to make a decision to do something, despite the way you feel, because that decision will help you become the man or woman you want to be. Serving others when you are very aware that you long to be served can be one of those decisions.

Be Intentional

Many people are willing and able to serve if the right opportunity comes along. If those opportunities don't present themselves, they just continue to do what they do. We find that serving requires more intentionality than that. You have to plan to serve, and seek out opportunities to do so.

One of the husbands we worked with came into our office one day with a chart. He was an accountant, and spread sheets, graphs, and charts were his "thing." So he had created a chart for himself to use in serving his wife. Down the left column were listed the seven desires. Across the page were listed the days of the week. At the beginning of the day he would look at his list and begin to plan ways in which he would listen to his wife. Every day he would look for ways to affirm her. He would think of actual things to say. He also made sure that he told his wife every day how much he loved her even if she hadn't done anything special for him. This man made sure that he helped with the children, kept the budget, worked hard at his job, and acted consistently in all of his behaviors. He wanted his wife to feel safe. Regularly he touched his wife, held her hand, and hugged her. She came to understand that this was not about his neediness, sexually or otherwise, but was just another of his ways to give. Every day he tried to compliment his wife on how she looked and how attractive he found her. Finally, every day he made time to tell her about his day, his experiences, his thoughts, and his feelings and to ask her about hers.

To be sure, he was not always successful in all of these ways every day. There were times when he was tired or irritable or frustrated or angry. But this man did make it a habit to look at this chart to see how well he had done checking the boxes. Surprisingly, he found that if he had gone a fairly long time — days — without doing any giving, it didn't mean he then immediately needed to give. Rather, it meant that he needed to examine how he was nurturing himself. His stress and tiredness meant he needed to rest or find recreation, to talk with friends, to do something he liked to do. Once he had nurtured himself, then he had something to give.

What this man was doing was seeking to find a healthy balance in his life. He loved his wife as he loved himself. He was intentional about it. By loving himself, he was able to love and serve for the right reason. He was not looking for anything back. His motivation was pure.

We encourage you to use the chart on pages 188–89 to intentionally serve others in your life. You may think of your children. Do you give them the seven desires — the yearnings that all children have — every day? You can serve your spouse, your parents, siblings, friends, employees and employers, strangers — and even God. As you intentionally work to serve everyone in this way, you are really practicing unconditional love.

Finally, be realistic. Don't take this chart and assume that you are going to do all of these acts of service every day for the rest of your life. We encourage you to do it for one day or one week. See

	Monday	Tuesday	Wednesday
Heard & Understood			
Affirmed			
Blessed: "I love you."			
Safe			
Healthy Touch			
Chosen			
Included			

Thursday	Friday	Saturday	Sunday

how it goes. If you practice in short-term ways, you may find that doing so becomes a regular habit. Thinking about the next year or the rest of your life can be overwhelming. Start small.

Giving is the most fulfilling activity that any of us can do. And those who give intentionally, with a purpose, and with the right motivation can serve and not grow weary.

Points to Ponder

- When you try to serve someone else when you are depleted and drained, how do you feel about the person and about yourself?

- Do you encourage people to share their stories with you? Do you share your stories with others?

- Who are you trying to serve today? Is your motivation pure?

- Is there anyone who is trying to serve you and you wish they wouldn't? What do you do to try and stop it?

- Who do you wish to serve intentionally?

TRUE CONTENTMENT

I have learned the secret of being content
in any and every situation, whether well fed or hungry,
whether living in plenty or in want.
PHILIPPIANS 4:11–12

We want to share with you our perspective on what brings true contentment in life. We hope that by reading this book up to this point, your ideas about contentment have already changed. Mainly, we hope that you are coming to know that contentment does not come externally through finding perfect relationships, acquiring material things, or having unique and exciting experiences. Contentment comes internally through our relationship with God, and it comes in fulfilling our own seven desires and the desires of others.

One of our favorite preachers is John Ortberg. We heard him preach a sermon about contentment, and he opened by comparing our drive for contentment to kids desperately wanting the next "Happy Meal." McDonald's has done a great marketing job creating the thought that a certain hamburger, French fries, and Coke combined with an interesting box and a toy will bring us happiness. Of course not too long after you've finished that joy-filled meal, the happiness wears off, and then you wait for your next one. The writer of Ecclesiastes puts it this way: "All man's efforts are for his mouth, yet his appetite is never satisfied" (Ecclesiastes 6:7). What satisfies your appetite?

Contentment is often defined in "if only" terms. If only we came from different families or life circumstances, then we'd be happy. If only we had more money, more friends, more success, more time off, a nicer car, a bigger house, or a faster computer. If only we had thought of that. If only we could play the piano, learn to fly, play professional baseball, become a doctor. If only we had a different job, lived in another place, or been born during a different time. If only our spouse was nicer to us, knew our love language, wanted sex more (or less) often, or didn't yell or criticize so much. If only we hadn't said that, done that, made that decision, or had some event happen to us. If only all of these things were true, then we would find contentment.

So what do you think would make you happy?

The truth is that there is no amount of fame or fortune — indeed, there are no life circumstances of any kind — that can make us content if we don't know the truth about who we are as God made us. But with knowledge of God and self-knowledge, we can experience contentment. Following are some ways to cultivate contentment.

Have Realistic Expectations

In chapter 4 we discussed expectations, where they come from, how they develop, and what we can do about them. One of the points to remember is that expectations can be totally unrealistic. We might expect our desires to be met from someone who has no ability to do so. We might have expectations that no one in the history of the world could meet. If you have based your feeling of contentment on unrealistic expectations, then you will never feel content. John Ortberg, in that same sermon we just mentioned, provided this wonderful equation for contentment: "Contentment equals reality minus expectations." Remember that unrealistic expectations will also foster anger and resentment, the polar opposite of contentment.

Even if expectations are realistic, they still may not be met. As we are writing this, we just returned from a Thanksgiving trip we had approached with many realistic expectations: we expected family members who said they were going to be there to be there; we expected flights to be on time; we expected weather to cooperate; we expected everyone to be in good health and humor; we expected that work schedules wouldn't disrupt our need to be together. Many of those expectations were not met. Our time together would have been ruined if we did not tolerate the unexpected. There are many times when we need to just let go of our expectations and allow the moment to be whatever it is. We find that when we can do that, there is always something meaningful that happens and something to enjoy.

Exchange Your Fantasies for Visions

Another word for unrealistic expectations is *fantasy*. A fantasy is a mental picture of the solution we think would heal all of our pain and satisfy all of our desires. There are many different kinds of fantasies: fame, money (and the things it can buy), success, power, status, romance, and sex. Fantasies can do one of two main things. They can recall past events that caused us pain and imagine a different result. They can also create pictures of us getting all of the things in life we think will satisfy our desires.

For example, when Mark was in high school he had a dream of becoming a professional tennis player. In the Illinois State High

School tennis tournament he played a young sophomore who would later go on to be one of the greatest tennis players of all time: Jimmy Connors. Mark was soundly defeated, and he somehow knew that if this short, young player could beat him so easily, he was probably not going to be the pro he dreamed of being. However, when Mark replays that match in his mind, he usually wins the game.

Mark used to think that if he was a tennis pro, people would like him and look up to him. When he wins that match in his mind, the fantasy brings to him lots of affirmation and a sense that he is really admired. This fantasy makes Mark feel pumped up for a little while, but it doesn't bring contentment.

Do you have financial fantasies? Perhaps you dream about winning the lottery and how all that money will bring you lots of things that will make you happy. Perhaps you fantasize about a job or position of power that will correct all your images of being a failure and of not providing the money you think you should. Fantasies can even get rather specific. Do any of you fantasize that if you drove a certain car, lived in a certain house, or wore certain clothes, people would really admire you? Romance fantasies bring a relationship into our minds that we think might solve all of our loneliness. Sexual fantasies can create images of all the affirmation, choosing, inclusion, or touch that we think we've never had or will not otherwise get.

Think about how the media and our advertising industry encourages us to create fantasies. They portray movie stars and other personalities who seem to be happy. Advertising shows us images of people who seem really content because they are using a certain product. These images are a lie. Mark has worked with many movie stars, rock stars, country and western stars, and professional athletes. He can attest to the fact that neither money, fame, power, nor the adulation of others have made these people content.

The mental images we put into our mind will determine what kind of images we will see in the world, and those images will determine our appetite. Recently Mark decided he wanted a new car. He decided on a particular make and model of car and put a mental image of that car into his mind. He then noticed every make and model of that car out on the road. Whatever mental images you put in your mind will create an appetite for those things. If you put pornographic images in your mind, it will create a lustful appetite. You will start seeing more sexual stimuli in the world. If you put images of fancy houses or fancy cars in your mind, you will see everyone out there who has those things. Do you "see" that what you think about determines what you see? And what you see will often determine what you do.

A vision, on the other hand, is a different mental picture, one that it is based on God's calling, plan, and purpose in our life. Everyone has such a calling, plan, and purpose, but how many of us search it out? The popularity of Rick Warren's book *The Purpose Driven Life* shows us that millions of people are interested in what that purpose is.[1] The Bible says, "Where there is no vision, the people perish" (Proverbs 29:18 KJV). When God puts a vision in our brain, we will develop a different appetite. We will "hunger and thirst after righteousness." Jesus says in Matthew 5:6, "Blessed are those who hunger and thirst for righteousness, for they will be filled."

When we operate out of a God-inspired vision, we will see opportunities to serve God by serving others. We encourage you to pursue your vision—and God's vision for you—in the following ways.

Follow Your Passion

What are you doing when you feel a real sense of joy and that you are doing something that you were meant to do? Don't listen to the voices of others about this, or voices from the present or the past. Listen to your own voice, and listen to God's voice. What do you think you're good at? Have you ever found something that you love doing and found that your creativity, productivity, and passion were limitless? Joy and passion are pretty good indicators that God is involved!

Tell Someone Else about Your Vision

It's always been amazing to us that when we have told people about our visions, our friends have had great ideas for us and have even shown us the path to accomplish our vision. For example, Mark got a vision that he was called to go to Germany and do a lecture in his field. The very next week he was sharing that vision with a colleague who knew a German psychologist who has a seminar business. Within six months, Mark was in Germany giving that seminar.

Refine Your Vision Based on Reality

Mark might have thought his tennis fantasies were visions, but the reality of his genetics and training suggested otherwise. Still, Mark did not have to entirely abandon tennis—he just refined his vision. Mark eventually earned money by teaching tennis while he was in graduate school.

Together we, Mark and Deb, believe that we have a vision to teach, preach, write, and counsel. A part of that vision was to build our own counseling center. We originally thought that this meant finding land and building a building. We dreamed of a log or timber frame building on some wooded site in an idyllic location. Eventually, we discovered how expensive land and building were and that any idyllic setting was going to be too far away for any of our clients to conveniently get to. Still, we continued to have a vision for a counseling center.

As we drove around our area of the country, we began to see many "for sale" signs on commercial buildings. Finally, we saw a sign for a complex of townhome-like buildings that were going to be used for offices. We were discouraged when we called because all of the units in this complex had been sold. When the builder heard about our vision, however, he decided to sell us the unit that he had reserved for himself.

We still didn't think we could afford it, but we told our vision to a friend who loves to help with creative financing. He outlined a very basic plan for us to buy this building. Today we own our counseling center, and we got to design it in a way that is consistent with our vision of a safe, comfortable counseling center.

Keep Your Vision Before You

This can be as simple as writing it down and putting it someplace, like on your refrigerator, so that you can see it regularly. You will be amazed by how doing something that basic will begin to help you think every day about ways to accomplish that vision. You will "see" opportunities. Even small decisions will be made based on whether or not the choice will enable your vision. There are lots of things we get asked to do and lots of things that we would like to do. Everything we decide to do is based on the simple question, "Does this honor our vision?"

Surround Yourself with Encouraging People

Our friend and colleague Eli Machen calls these people "vision stokers." There will always be people in your life who are naysayers. They will tell you, "That is too hard or impossible. You'll never do that." There are, however, people who sense your passion and enthusiasm and will encourage that. They will say, "That really sounds inspired" or "That really seems to be of God. Go for it." As we said, these may very well be the people who help you find the ways to get it done.

When you follow a vision, you will find contentment. When you are aligned with God's plan and purpose, life will have harmony and rhythm. What could be better?

Cultivate Gratitude

Have you not heard that contentment comes from a sense of gratitude for the things or circumstances that we have? The old phrase, "an attitude of gratitude," is really descriptive of feeling content. We Americans have a national day of Thanksgiving and are forced at least once a year to think about things that we're thankful for. It is easy to say, "Be thankful" or "Let's give thanks," but in the midst of our sorrows and problems, being thankful is not always easy. Still, the more we practice gratitude, the more natural gratitude seems. Try making a daily or weekly list of five things for which you are thankful. At first it might seem hard, but the more you do it, the easier it gets.

Sometimes being grateful is about focusing on what is good or truthful, even in the midst of other factors that are not so good. We can so easily become detectives who only search out every detail of what is going wrong. Paul reminds us to think positive when he writes, "Whatever is true, whatever is noble, whatever is right, whatever is pure, whatever is lovely, whatever is admirable—if anything is excellent or praiseworthy—think about such things" (Philippians 4:8).

Recognize that your purpose will often flow out of your pain. And thus, we come full circle. We have taken you from looking at the pain that emerges from living in an imperfect world that cannot always give you your desires, to recognizing the pain of those losses, to finding the purpose that can be found in surrendering that pain to God.

Throughout this book we have told you stories of many different people. Some of those situations resonated with you. Others may have been unfamiliar. We would like you to know that whatever your problems are, the principles of this book are effective. From the simplest of problems to the most complex, they work.

The following story is one of the most painful stories that we have ever heard. We share it with you in the hope that you will know that there is nothing so painful that God cannot transform it. It is a story about a beautiful little girl named Shelly.

Shelly was severely abused as a little girl: verbally abused by her mom, physically abused by her mom and brothers, and sexually abused by her priest. When she came to therapy to face all the pain of what she had lost in life and the desires that had never been filled, she was profoundly sad and angry. But in the months that followed, she moved through that pain to find her comfort in serving young women who were also abused. And she used the coping that she had learned so well—singing—to help her survive. Today she leads a choir of over sixty young women, with proceeds that support ministries for abused girls all over the world. She is finding as she serves those girls that she is being served the desires of her heart by the girls, by herself, by her family, and by God.

Shelly has shared in a lengthy email to us some of the spiritual journey that she has been on as she has faced the losses of the seven desires in her youth and sometimes can't find even in her committed and loving marriage. She has given us permission to use her words:

> [My husband] Mark and I have been struggling so much lately. I realize that I do think God is trying to teach me so

much about letting Mark "be" (even though I need him so desperately to be there for me right now). I am understanding his pain, his loss, his little eyes as a boy. This doesn't mean that I am not frustrated. It seems that I am getting to the heart of Jesus in all of my emotions and pain. I am able to hold anger, frustration, and acceptance with love at the same time. I have to think that Jesus felt the same things on the cross ... well, throughout his entire life here on earth, yet he lived without sin.

I wonder why God had me go through all of this.... I believe I am being shown what his divine love looks like for me by being allowed to experience this. I have to ask God what is it that he wants me to get. "Teach me how to love like you do." I am asking God what is it that he wants me to do with my life with all of what he has shown me. This contentedness I find in the midst of my deep weeping is one that I know you understand. It gives me in my flesh a chance to begin to start to think that someday I will realize that what I have been given here on this earth is truly enough. Without the pain, the world just seems to go by without any real existence.

We have asked you to think about your life, your expectations, and the fantasies you have had about what will make you happy. We hope that you won't go in search of the next "happy meal." The true banquet of life is not in those external hopes but in your internal knowledge of God and his plan and will for your life.

Finally ...

Reading a book like this is never an end in itself. If all you ever do is read books, your life will not be transformed. We hope that reading this book has inspired you to think about how God has empowered you to live a different, more fulfilling life—regardless of your circumstances or relationships. We pray that you will embrace the truths about who you are: that you are fearfully and wonderfully made, a beloved child of God, a unique treasure who is worthy to be valued. From this truthful place, may you be able to let go of the many unhealthy ways you have coped to comfort yourself. Instead of trusting life or others to provide the seven desires of your heart, you will turn to the only one who can—God.

SUGGESTED READING

Brain Chemistry

Amen, Daniel. *Change Your Brain, Change Your Life.* New York: Times Books, 1998.

Milkman, Harvey and Stanley Sunderwirth. *Craving for Ecstasy: The Consciousness and Chemistry of Escape.* Lexington, Mass.: Lexington Press, 1987.

Codependency

Beattie, Melody. *Beyond Codependency.* New York: Harper/Hazelden, 1989.

———. *Codependents' Guide to the Twelve Steps.* New York: Simon & Schuster, 1990.

———. *Codependent No More.* New York: Harper/Hazelden, 1987.

Mellody, Pia. *Facing Codependence.* New York: HarperSanFrancisco, 1989.

Subby, Robert. *Lost in the Shuffle.* Deerfield Beach, Fla.: Health Communications, 1987.

Couples Relationship

Bader, Ellyn and Peter Pearson. *In Quest of the Mythical Mate*. New York: Brunner/Mazel, 1988.

Carnes, Patrick, Debra Laaser, and Mark Laaser. *Open Hearts: Renewing Relationships with Recovery, Romance, and Reality*. Wickenburg, Ariz.: Gentle Path Press, 1999.

Clinton, Tim. *Before a Bad Goodbye*. Nashville: Word, 1999.

Hendrix, Harville. *Getting the Love You Want*. New York: Henry Holt, 1988.

Hybels, Bill and Lynne. *Fit to Be Tied*. Grand Rapids, Mich.: Zondervan, 1991.

Laaser, Debra. *Shattered Vows*. Grand Rapids, Mich.: Zondervan, 2008.

Thomas, Gary. *Sacred Marriage*. Grand Rapids, Mich.: Zondervan, 2000.

Families

Bradshaw, John. *Healing the Shame That Binds You*. Deerfield Beach, Fla.: Health Communications, 1988.

———. *Homecoming*. New York: Bantam Books, 1990.

Friel, John and Linda. *Adult Children: The Secrets of Dysfunctional Families*. Deerfield Beach, Fla.: Health Communications, 1988.

———. *An Adult Child's Guide to What's Normal*. Deerfield Beach, Fla.: Health Communications, 1990.

Smalley, Gary and John Trent. *The Blessing*. Nashville: Thomas Nelson, 1986.

Whitfield, Charles. *Healing the Child Within*. Deerfield Beach, Fla.: Health Communications, 1987.

Healthy Sexuality

Hart, Archibald, Catherine Hart Weber, Debra Taylor. *Secrets of Eve*. Nashville: Word, 1998.

Hart, Archibald. *The Sexual Man*. Dallas: Word, 1994.

Laaser, Mark. *Healing the Wounds of Sexual Addiction*. Grand Rapids, Mich.: Zondervan, 2004.

———. *Talking to Your Kids about Sex*. Colorado Springs: Water-Brook, 1999.

Maltz, Wendy. *The Sexual Healing Journey*. New York: Harper Perennial, 1992.

Penner, Cliff and Joyce. *Restoring the Pleasure*. Dallas: Word, 1993.

Rosenau, Doug. *A Celebration of Sex*. Nashville: Thomas Nelson, 1994.

General

Cloud, Henry and John Townsend. *Boundaries*. Grand Rapids, Mich.: Zondervan, 1992.

———. *How People Grow*. Grand Rapids, Mich.: Zondervan, 2001.

———. *Safe People*. Grand Rapids, Mich.: Zondervan, 1995.

Hart, Archibald. *Adrenaline and Stress*. Nashville: W, 1995.

———. *The Anxiety Cure*. Nashville: W, 1999.

Hart, Archibald and Catherine Hart Weber. *Unveiling Depression in Women*. Grand Rapids, Mich.: Fleming H. Revell, 2002.

Hemfelt, Robert, Frank Minirth, and Paul Meier. *Love Is a Choice*. Nashville: Thomas Nelson, 1989.

Lerner, Harriet. *The Dance of Anger*. New York: Harper, 1985.

———. *The Dance of Connection.* New York: Harper, 2001.

———. *The Dance of Intimacy.* New York: HarperCollins, 1990.

May, Gerald. *Addiction and Grace.* New York: Harper, 1988.

Peck, M. Scott. *The Road Less Traveled.* New York: Simon & Schuster, 1978.

Stoop, David. *Forgiving the Unforgivable.* Ann Arbor, Mich.: Servant, 2001.

Swenson, Richard. *Margin: Restoring Emotional, Physical, Financial, and Time Reserves to Overloaded Lives.* Colorado Springs: NavPress, 2004.

Wilson, Sandra. *Released from Shame: Recovery for Adult Children of Dysfunctional Families.* Downers Grove, Ill.: InterVarsity, 1990.

Inspirational

Chambers, Oswald. *My Utmost for His Highest.* Uhrichsville, Ohio: Barbour, 1963.

Crabb, Larry. *Shattered Dreams: God's Unexpected Pathway to Joy.* Colorado Springs: WaterBrook, 2001.

Kendall, R. T. *Total Forgiveness.* Lake Mary, Fla.: Charisma House, 2002.

Kidd, Sue Monk. *When the Heart Waits.* New York: HarperCollins, 1990.

Nouwen, Henri. *The Inner Voice of Love: A Journey Through Anguish to Freedom.* New York: Image Books, 1996.

———. *Life of the Beloved.* New York: Crossroad, 1992.

———. *The Return of the Prodigal Son.* New York: Image Books, 1994.

Ortberg, John. *Everybody's Normal Till You Get to Know Them.* Grand Rapids, Mich.: Zondervan, 2003.

———. *If You Want to Walk on Water, You've Got to Get Out of the Boat.* Grand Rapids, Mich.: Zondervan, 2001.

———. *Love Beyond Reason.* Grand Rapids, Mich.: Zondervan, 1998.

The Journey of Recovery: A New Testament. Colorado Springs: International Bible Society, 2006.

Warren, Rick. *The Purpose Driven Life.* Grand Rapids, Mich.: Zondervan, 2002.

Wilkinson, Bruce. *The Dream Giver.* Sisters, Ore.: Multnomah, 2003.

Wilson, Sandra. *Into Abba's Arms: Finding the Acceptance You've Always Wanted.* Wheaton, Ill.: Tyndale, 1998.

Meditation Books

Answers in the Heart: Daily Meditations for Men and Women Recovering from Sex Addiction. San Francisco: Harper/Hazelden, 1989.

Casey, Karen. *Each Day a New Beginning: Daily Meditations for Women.* San Francisco: Hazelden, 2006.

———. *Some Days: Notes from the Heart of Recovery.* New York: Harper & Row, 1990.

Hemfelt, Robert and Fowler. *Serenity: A Companion for Twelve Step Recovery.* Nashville: Thomas Nelson, 1990.

Schaef, Anne Wilson. *Meditations for Women Who Do Too Much.* New York: HarperCollins, 1990.

Sexual and Emotional Abuse

Adams, Kenneth M. *Silently Seduced: Understanding Covert Incest.* Deerfield Beach, Fla.: Health Communications, 1991.

Allender, Dan B. *The Wounded Heart.* Colorado Springs: NavPress, 1990.

Bass, Ellen and Laura Davis. *The Courage to Heal.* New York: Harper & Row, 1988.

Friberg, Nils C. and Mark Laaser. *Before the Fall: Preventing Pastoral Sexual Abuse.* Collegeville, Minn.: Liturgical, 1998.

Hopkins, Nancy Myer and Mark Laaser, eds. *Restoring the Soul of a Church: Congregations Wounded by Clergy Sexual Misconduct.* Collegeville, Minn.: Liturgical, 1995.

Hunter, Mic. *Abused Boys: The Neglected Victims of Sexual Abuse.* New York: Fawcett, 1991.

Langberg, Diane. *On the Threshold of Hope.* Wheaton, Ill.: Tyndale House, 1999.

Lew, Mike. *Victims No Longer: Men Recovering from Incest and Other Sexual Child Abuse.* New York: Harper & Row, 1990.

Love, Patricia. *Emotional Incest Syndrome.* New York: Bantam Books, 1990.

Spiritual Abuse

Arterburn, Stephen and Jack Felton. *Toxic Faith.* Colorado Springs: WaterBrook, 1991, 2001.

Johnson, David and Jeff VanVonderen. *Subtle Power of Spiritual Abuse.* Bloomington, Minn.: Bethany House, 2005.

Virginia Satir

Andreas, Steve. *Virginia Satir: The Patterns of Her Magic.* Palo Alto, Calif.: Science and Behavior Books, 1991.

Loeschen, Sharon. *Enriching Your Relationship with Yourself and Others.* Burien, Washington: AVANTA The Virginia Satir Network, 2005.

Satir, Virginia. *Conjoint Family Therapy.* Palo Alto, Calif.: Science and Behavior Books, 1983.

———. *The New People Making.* Palo Alto, Calif.: Science and Behavior Books, 1988.

Satir, Virginia and Michele Baldwin. *Satir Step by Step.* Palo Alto, Calif.: Science and Behavior Books, 1983.

Satir, Virginia, John Banmen, Jane Gerber, and Maria Gomori. *The Satir Model: Family Therapy and Beyond.* Palo Alto, Calif.: Science and Behavior Books, 1991.

NOTES

Introduction

1. Mark's story about his sexual addiction can be found in his book *Healing the Wounds of Sexual Addiction* (Grand Rapids, Mich.: Zondervan, 2004). Debbie's story of how she dealt with Mark's addiction can be found in her book *Shattered Vows* (Grand Rapids, Mich.: Zondervan, 2008).

Chapter 1: The Seven Desires

1. See Mark's book *Healing the Wounds of Sexual Addiction* (Grand Rapids, Mich.: Zondervan, 2004).

Chapter 2: The Problem Is Not the Problem

1. Virginia Satir, *Peoplemaking* (Palo Alto, Calif.: Science and Behavior Books, 1972), 3.

2. Adapted from Virginia Satir, John Banmen, Jane Gerber, and Maria Gomori, *The Satir Model: Family Therapy and Beyond* (Palo Alto, Calif.: Science & Behavior Books, 1991).

Chapter 3: The Truth about Who You Are

1. Most of the material in this chart was also published in Mark Laaser, *Healing the Wounds of Sexual Addiction* (Grand Rapids, Mich.: Zondervan, 2004), 95.

2. Ibid, 95.

Chapter 4: Expectations: The Pathway to Anger and Resentment

1. *Webster's Dictionary of Synonyms & Antonyms* (New York: Smithmark, 1996).

2. *Webster's New World Thesaurus.*

Chapter 5: Perceptions, Meanings, and Core Beliefs

1. Pat Love and Jo Robinson, *Hot Monogamy* (New York: Penguin Putnam, 1995), 72–73.

2. Campbell Leaper and Melanie Ayres, "A Meta-Analytic Review of Gender Variations in Adults' Language Use: Talkativeness, Affiliative Speech and Assertive Speech," *Personality and Social Psychology Review*, November 2007.

Chapter 6: Feelings — And Feelings about Feelings

1. *The American Heritage Dictionary* (New York: Houghton Mifflin, 1983).

2. Tim Clinton—plenary speech, AACC World Conference 2003.

Chapter 8: Coping in Relationship

1. Artwork for stances by Mary P. Munger

Chapter 10: Triggers as Transformations

1. Henri Nouwen, *The Inner Voice of Love* (New York: Random House, 1998), 103.

2. Frederick Buechner, *Wishful Thinking* (San Francisco: HarperSanFrancisco, 1993), 2.

Chapter 12: Fulfilling Your Own Desires

1. Satir Training in Atlanta with Maureen Graves, November 2007.

Chapter 14: True Contentment

1. Rick Warren, *The Purpose Driven Life* (Grand Rapids, Mich.: Zondervan, 2000).

How to Contact Us

Mark and Debbie Laaser

Faithful & True Ministries

15798 Venture Lane

Eden Prairie, Minnesota

FTMinistries@aol.com

www.faithfulandtrueministries.com

www.7DesiresofEveryHeart.com

Healing the Wounds of Sexual Addiction

Dr. Mark R. Laaser,
Founder of Faithful and True Ministries

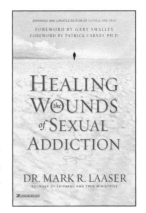

"Mark has eloquently unraveled the mystery behind addictive behavior: when our relationships are not alive and growing, the temptation for various kinds of addictions is unleashed."
— Dr. Gary Smalley

With today's rampant availability of Internet pornography, sexual addiction has become a national epidemic that affects up to 10 percent of Christians. As devastating as any drug habit, it brings heartbreak and despair to those it entangles. But there is help for men and women caught in sexual addiction's downward spiral.

This book offers a path that leads beyond compulsive thoughts and behaviors to healing and transformation. Sensitive to the shame of sexual addiction without minimizing its sinfulness, Dr. Mark Laaser traces the roots of the problem, discusses its patterns and impact, and maps out a biblical approach to self-control and sexual integrity.

Previously titled *Faithful and True*, this revision includes an all-new section that deals with sexual addiction in the church. Other important changes reflect cultural trends, incorporate current research, and place a greater emphasis on spiritual growth. This book also addresses the unique needs and issues of female sex addicts.

Whether you know someone with a sexual addiction or struggle yourself, *Healing the Wounds of Sexual Addiction* points the way to understanding, wholeness, and holiness.

Softcover 978-0-310-25657-1

Pick up a copy today at your favorite bookstore!

Shattered Vows

Hope and Healing for Women Who Have Been Sexually Betrayed

Debra Laaser

Infidelity doesn't have to ruin your life —
or your marriage

If you have been devastated by your husband's sexual betrayal — whether an isolated incident or a long-term pattern of addiction — you need to know you don't have to live as a victim. If you choose to stay in your marriage, you have options other than punishing, tolerating, or ignoring your spouse; in fact, extraordinary growth awaits a woman willing to deal with the pain of her husband's struggles with sexual purity. Even if a spouse will not participate in a program for healing, a woman who has been sexually betrayed can change her own life in powerful and permanent ways.

This sensitive guide provides practical tools to help you make wise and empowering decisions, emotional tools to develop greater intimacy in your life, and spiritual tools to transform your suffering. Debra Laaser's personal journey through betrayal, her extensive work with hundreds of hurting women, and her intimate marriage two decades after the disclosure of her husband's infidelity provide meaningful answers to the questions that arise amid the complex fallout of broken vows.

The pain endured from sexual betrayal can break your heart, but it does not need to break your life.

Softcover 978-0-310-27394-3

Pick up a copy today at your favorite bookstore!

Share Your Thoughts

With the Author: Your comments will be forwarded to the author when you send them to *zauthor@zondervan.com*.

With Zondervan: Submit your review of this book by writing to *zreview@zondervan.com*.

Free Online Resources at
www.zondervan.com/hello

 Zondervan AuthorTracker: Be notified whenever your favorite authors publish new books, go on tour, or post an update about what's happening in their lives.

 Daily Bible Verses and Devotions: Enrich your life with daily Bible verses or devotions that help you start every morning focused on God.

 Free Email Publications: Sign up for newsletters on fiction, Christian living, church ministry, parenting, and more.

 Zondervan Bible Search: Find and compare Bible passages in a variety of translations at www.zondervanbiblesearch.com.

 Other Benefits: Register yourself to receive online benefits like coupons and special offers, or to participate in research.